# Sci-Fi Directors

Craig E. Blohm

San Diego, CA

© 2017 ReferencePoint Press, Inc.
Printed in the United States

**For more information, contact:**
ReferencePoint Press, Inc.
PO Box 27779
San Diego, CA 92198
www.ReferencePointPress.com

LIBRARY OF CONGRESS CATALOGING-IN-PUBLICATION DATA

Name: Blohm, Craig E., 1948-
Title: Sci-Fi Directors/by Craig E. Blohm.
Description: San Diego, CA : ReferencePoint Press, Inc., 2016. | Series:
  Collective biographies | Includes bibliographical references and index.
Identifiers: LCCN 2015046497 (print) | LCCN 2015048288 (ebook) | ISBN
  9781682820308 (hardback) | ISBN 9781682820315 (epub)
Subjects: LCSH: Motion picture producers and directors--Biography. | Science
  fiction films--History and criticism.
Classification: LCC PN1998.2 B585 2016 (print) | LCC PN1998.2 (ebook) | DDC
  791.4302/330922--dc23
LC record available at http://lccn.loc.gov/2015046497

# CONTENTS

# The World of Science Fiction

**S**ix astronomers flew to the moon in a bullet-shaped space capsule in 1902. There they battled an alien race called the Selenites and returned triumphantly to Earth. Of course, this trip was pure fiction—*science* fiction. And it was created in the then-new medium of film. The fourteen-minute French production, entitled *La Voyage Dans la Lune* (*A Trip to the Moon*), is considered the first science fiction movie. It was directed by magician and filmmaker George Méliès, who created special effects to take his audiences on a fanciful journey beyond Earth. But Méliès was not the first to combine science with fiction.

## The Origins of Science Fiction

Science fiction has been notoriously difficult to define. Isaac Asimov, one of the most celebrated science fiction authors, describes it as "that branch of literature that deals with human responses to changes in the level of science and technology."[1] As scientific knowledge advanced during the eighteenth and nineteenth centuries, so did the use of science themes in fiction.

*Frankenstein*, written by British author Mary Shelley in 1816, is often thought of as simply a monster story, partly due to its reincarnation in numerous twentieth-century films. But it is usually considered the first true science fiction novel, centering around a doctor using science to create life.

Other European authors began to see the potential for drama in science-based fiction. In the late nineteenth century, French author Jules Verne wrote the popular novels *Twenty Thousand Leagues Under the Sea* and *Journey to the Center of the Earth.* Known at the time as *scientific romances*, these classic works convey the wonder of strange places and take their characters on fantastic adventures, relying on the scientific knowledge of the day to lend authenticity to the stories. In 1901 British author H.G. Wells published *The First Men in the Moon*, which inspired Méliès to create his film. Wells's other classic novels, *The War of the Worlds, The Invisible Man*, and *The Time Machine*, were each made into films. So important are Wells's works that literary critic Patrick Parrender has called him "the pivotal figure in the evolution of scientific romance into modern science fiction."[2]

"[Science fiction is] that branch of literature that deals with human responses to changes in the level of science and technology."[1]

—Science fiction author Isaac Asimov

## Science Fiction in Film

In the early-twentieth century, science fiction made the leap from the page to the screen. In 1927 German filmmaker Fritz Lang directed *Metropolis*, a feature-length science fiction movie that had an immense influence on future sci-fi films. The film's iconic golden robot has become a symbol of early sci-fi cinema, and it was an inspiration for the *Star Wars* droid C-3PO.

By the 1950s sci-fi films had become a part of pop culture. Most midcentury sci-fi films were considered B movies—meaning low-budget productions featuring rubber-suited monsters and crude special effects. But some films were a cut above the rest

*In addition to having the skill to capture futuristic worlds on camera, sci-fi directors must also possess the imagination necessary to envision how those worlds will look. To bring the future to life, they collaborate chiefly with set designers, prop makers, and their directors of photography.*

and employed science fiction as social commentary. This was especially true during the Cold War of the 1950s and 1960s, when the fear of nuclear war was all too real. In the 1951 film *The Day the Earth Stood Still*, a peaceful alien comes to Earth to warn against the spread of nuclear weapons. *Invasion of the Body Snatchers*, a 1956 sci-fi classic, is the story of aliens taking over human bodies, turning them into so-called pod people devoid of emotion and individuality. Reviewers interpreted the film's theme either as a warning against social conformity or the threat of a Communist takeover of American society.

As America prepared to land a man on the moon and public interest in space travel grew, science fiction films gradually gained a new measure of respect—beginning with the groundbreaking 1968 film *2001: A Space Odyssey*. Blockbusters such as *Star Wars*, *Alien*, and *Avatar* ushered in a new type of science fiction film experience—introducing alien worlds of complexity and realism with the help of technology that created special effects more spectacular, yet believable, than ever before. By the twenty-first century, science fiction films were among the most daring of cinematic ventures and were immensely profitable at the box office.

## Directors at the Helm

Behind every one of these films is a director who applies his unique vision to a screenplay and realizes that vision by directing the characters and action of the film. (In recent memory, nearly all directors in the science fiction genre have been men.) Directing a science fiction movie takes talent and discipline; it also requires the ability to boldly imagine a future that might one day (or never) come to pass. Few directors can manage such a daunting task, but those who do inspire, thrill, and delight their audiences with the wonders of things to come.

# CHAPTER 1

# Steven Spielberg

**A** brilliant searchlight beam stabbed the darkening sky over the Phoenix Little Theater as moviegoers filed through the doors to attend the premiere of a new science fiction movie. The theater's marquee proclaimed the film's title in bold letters: *Firelight*. For more than two hours, the audience watched as UFOs zoomed across the screen, menacing the film's young actors who appeared appropriately terrified. It was March 14, 1964, and *Firelight* was the first feature-length movie directed by a seventeen-year-old with an all-consuming interest in filmmaking. That teenage director was Steven Spielberg, and his hobby would ultimately make him one of the most celebrated directors in Hollywood.

Steven Allan Spielberg was born in Cincinnati, Ohio, on December 18, 1946, the first child of parents Arnold, an engineer who worked on developing early computers, and Leah, a concert pianist. His father's occupation required the Spielberg family to relocate, first from Ohio to New Jersey, and then in 1957, when Steven was ten years old, to Phoenix, Arizona. Being uprooted had a lasting effect on the young Spielberg. "Just as I'd become accustomed to a school and a teacher and a best friend, the

FOR SALE sign would dig into the front lawn." He longed for the stability of a typical suburban lifestyle, a yearning that he would later express in many of his films. Spielberg learned a strong work ethic from his father, but frequent business trips distanced Arnold from his son. "I always felt my father put his work before me . . . and I suffered as a result."[3] It was understandable, then, that Spielberg became closer to his mother, who was outgoing, creative, and always there for him.

Life in Phoenix was uncomfortable at times. The Spielbergs were one of only a few Jewish families living there. Steven often felt like an outsider. "Being a Jew meant that I was not normal," he recalls. "I was not like everybody else. I just wanted to be accepted."[4] Another barrier to acceptance was his appearance. Spielberg was a gawky kid with big ears and a prominent nose. He was the nerd who tried hard but did not do well at sports. What he did do well, however, was tell stories, usually scary ones, to his three younger sisters. It was a talent that he would build into a successful film career.

## The Budding Filmmaker

Spielberg found a new outlet for his storytelling soon after his family moved to Phoenix. His father had received an eight-millimeter movie camera as a gift, and Steven used it to document camping trips and other family outings. He soon graduated from simply documenting reality to creating it in his films. His first film, shot when he was twelve, was *The Last Train Wreck*, a short disaster film that featured two model trains crashing into each other. Spielberg's next film, a western he called *The Last Gunfight*, earned him a Boy Scout photography merit badge and the applause of his fellow scouts who had acted in the film. After his western, in 1961 Spielberg tackled World War II with *Fighter Squad*, a fifteen-minute action movie featuring real P-51 fighter planes that he filmed on the ground at the local airport. The realism was astonishing for a no-budget film made by a fifteen-year-old boy. That same year another Spielberg war film, *Escape to Nowhere*, won first prize in the statewide Canyon Films Junior Film Festival.

*Steven Spielberg is a world-famous director of such science fiction blockbusters as* E.T.: The Extra-Terrestrial *and* Close Encounters of the Third Kind. *His interest in bringing such stories to the screen began when he was a teenager, directing his first sci-fi film while still in high school.*

In his western and his war films, Spielberg had explored America's past. With his next film, *Firelight*, he tried his hand at science fiction. The premiere at the Phoenix Little Theater was a rousing success, and the film made a profit—exactly one dollar, as Spielberg himself recalls. But it was the film's only showing. The next day the Spielberg family headed for California, with a new job for Steven's father and a new world of filmmaking for the promising director.

## Turning Pro

The Spielbergs settled in Saratoga, California, a small town located in what would become the high-tech region known as Silicon Valley. Steven attended Saratoga High School, where he experienced some incidents of bullying and anti-Semitism. These were not the only stresses on the young Spielberg, however; at home, his family was rapidly falling apart. Arnold and Leah's marriage had been troubled for several years, creating a subtle but palpable tension that upset the four Spielberg children. Soon after Steven graduated from Saratoga in June 1965, his parents separated and his father moved to Los Angeles. "My mom and dad split, and there was no longer a routine to follow. My life changed radically. I left home and went to L.A."[5] Steven lived with his father during his first year of college at California State University in Long Beach. The Spielbergs' divorce became final in 1967. Family problems and suburban alienation would become recurring themes in Spielberg's later films.

In 1968 Spielberg completed his first professional film. *Amblin'* was a twenty-six-minute movie that depicted the travels of a young couple as they hitchhiked their way to the Pacific coast. The film won several awards, but more importantly, it led to Spielberg's first studio contract. Sidney Sheinberg, the head of production for television at Universal Studios, was impressed enough by *Amblin'* that he signed Spielberg to a seven-year directing deal. Spielberg's first job was a segment of the television horror series *Night Gallery*, where he directed legendary Hollywood actress Joan Crawford. Looking even younger than his twenty-two years, Spielberg eventually overcame some initial mocking from the veteran crew and filmed the segment with his own visual style, using artistic shots and fluid camera movements.

Spielberg directed several more episodes of television shows and several television movies, but his dream had always been to direct feature films. In 1975 Spielberg made a big splash on the big screen.

> "My mom and dad split, and there was no longer a routine to follow. My life changed radically. I left home and went to L.A."[5]
>
> —Steven Spielberg

## Shark Fins

The year 1975 will be remembered as the year of the shark, thanks to Spielberg's watershed movie, *Jaws*. Selected as the film's director in 1973, Spielberg felt he could have fun with the story of a great white shark menacing a New England coastal resort town. Little did he realize the problems he would face. Shooting on the Atlantic Ocean off Martha's Vineyard, Massachusetts, was a nightmare of weather delays and the difficulty of shooting on bobbing boats. Even worse, the film's shark (actually three mechanical sharks), constantly broke down. With his main villain unavailable for long periods, Spielberg decided to film scenes that hinted at the shark's presence without showing it. This turned out to be a blessing in disguise, as it created an atmosphere of suspense and anticipation. By the time the shark appeared, audiences had been suitably unnerved and reacted with frightened screams.

*Jaws* became a smash hit when it was released in the summer of 1975, making over $100 million in its first two months, the most money made by any film to that time. It forever changed Hollywood as the first summer blockbuster movie, prompting studios to turn out spectacular films each year to lure people from the beaches to the theaters. *Jaws* established Spielberg's reputation as the brightest and most bankable of Hollywood's young directors and gave him the influence within the industry to make just about any film he wished. For his next project, Spielberg chose to explore the world of science fiction.

> "For me [*Close Encounters of the Third Kind* is] one of the most hopeful movies I've written and directed."[6]
>
> —*Steven Spielberg*

## Encountering UFOs

Sci-fi movies of the 1950s usually portrayed aliens as terrifying monsters bent on wiping out human civilization. In Spielberg's classic 1977 film *Close Encounters of the Third Kind*, he presented aliens as benevolent creatures who initiate contact with the human race. "For me," Spielberg recalls, "it's one of the most hopeful movies I've written and directed."[6]

In the film, electrical lineman Roy Neary becomes obsessed with images of a mountain that aliens have implanted in his

# Falling Stars over Phoenix

Soon after moving to Phoenix, an incident occurred that sparked young Spielberg's imagination and set him on a course toward creating his first sci-fi movie, *Firelight*.

One night my dad woke me up in the middle of the night and rushed me into our car in my night clothes. I didn't know what was happening. It was frightening. . . . He had a thermos of coffee and had brought blankets, and we drove for about half an hour. We finally pulled over onto the side of the road, and there were a couple hundred people, lying on their backs in the middle of the night, looking up at the sky. My dad found a place, spread the blanket out, and we both lay down.

He pointed to the sky, and there was a magnificent meteor shower. All these incredible points of light were crisscrossing the sky. It was a phenomenal display, apparently announced in advance by the weather bureau. My dad had really surprised me—actually he'd frightened the hell out of me! At the same time, though, I was tremendously attracted to the source, to what was causing this. . . .

[My dad] gave me a technical explanation of what was happening. . . . But I didn't want to hear that. I wanted to think of them as falling stars.

Quoted in Joseph McBride, *Steven Spielberg: A Biography.* Jackson: University Press of Mississippi, 2010, p. 68.

mind. Upon learning that the mountain really exists, he and a friend, whose son has been taken by the aliens, drive cross-country to see it. There they discover a secret government landing area for UFOs. When a huge alien craft finally lands, it is a spectacular event, reuniting mother and son and returning to Earth many others who had been abducted by UFOs over the years.

*Close Encounters of the Third Kind* was a remaking of Spielberg's first sci-fi movie, *Firelight*, but with state-of-the-art special effects. The suburbs and broken families, typical Spielberg themes, add humanity to the visual wonders of the film. Neary, bored with his everyday existence, exhibits an innocent sense of wonder as he encounters the aliens. The aliens themselves are childlike beings who eagerly bond with the humans who have

*Unlike many of the alien-invasion movies of the 1950s and 1960s, Steven Spielberg's* Close Encounters of the Third Kind *portrayed aliens as curious visitors willing to make peaceful contact with humanity. Here, the aliens come out of their craft to interact with human greeters.*

welcomed them to Earth. Eventually Neary leaves with the UFO when it departs Earth, abandoning his ordinary life forever.

*Close Encounters of the Third Kind* eventually made over $300 million and earned Spielberg his first Academy Award nomination for best director. Although he did not win the Oscar, he was pleased with his film: "I got what I wanted: Man's first contact with an extraterrestrial is formal, gentle, and a little strange."[7]

## Marriage and Faith

During the casting of the lead female role for *Close Encounters* in 1976, Spielberg met a twenty-two-year-old actress named Amy Irving. Although too young for the part, Irving caught Spielberg's eye and soon they were living together. After nearly four turbulent years, the two parted ways, only to reunite in 1984 and marry the next year. Career pressures again doomed the couple, and in 1989 they divorced. Spielberg later met actress Kate Capshaw, and they wed in 1991.

For years Spielberg's Jewish faith had remained dormant. It was Capshaw who led him back to the Judaism of his forebears. "Kate is Protestant," Spielberg explains, "and she insisted on converting to Judaism. . . . I think *that*, more than anything else, brought me back to Judaism."[8] One result of Spielberg's newly rediscovered faith was his 1993 film *Schindler's List*—based on the true story of a German businessman who risked his life to protect his Jewish workers from Nazi persecution during World War II. The film was a critical and box-office success. *Schindler's List* revealed Spielberg's ability to connect with his Jewish heritage and display that heritage on the screen in a poignant and powerful way.

Another legacy of Spielberg's rediscovery of his Jewish heritage is the Shoah Foundation, which he established at the University of Southern California in 1994. The foundation is a nonprofit organization dedicated to recording the stories of Jewish survivors of the Shoah, or Holocaust—the Nazi genocide of more than 6 million Jews during World War II. (*Shoah* is the modern Hebrew word for "catastrophe.") Spielberg also created the Righteous Persons Foundation, which has donated over $100 million in support of Jewish causes.

# Calling E.T.

Such serious films as *Schindler's List* were still in Spielberg's future as he continued to create science fiction movies that captured audiences' imagination and sense of wonder. If the aliens in *Close Encounters* were gentle and friendly, the extraterrestrial featured in Spielberg's next science fiction film was positively adorable. Spielberg's 1982 hit, *E.T. the Extra-Terrestrial*, tells the story of a UFO landing and a small alien accidentally left behind, confused and alone, when the craft hastily departs. The squat, large-eyed creature is befriended by Elliott, a ten-year-old boy who also feels lonely due to his absent father. The two unlikely friends come to share an emotional and psychic bond. When government authorities come after E.T. for scientific experimentation, the alien succumbs to an earthly illness. Elliott's connection with his alien friend revives E.T. After helping E.T. return to his own planet, Elliott stays behind, sad but a little more grown up.

# Spielberg the Storyteller

As the future director of such memorable movies as *Jurassic Park* and *War of the Worlds*, Spielberg showed an early talent for storytelling. Jane MacDonald Morley, one of Spielberg's New Jersey neighbors, recalls his fondness for relating scary tales:

On lazy summer afternoons when we were bored, we'd sit in the shade at the side of our house, five or six kids, and Stevie would be the one telling the stories. He always seemed to get the attention of the kids. The younger kids believed what Stevie said, because he was a good storyteller. . . . It was out of those sessions that the bogeyman story came. He told me "The bogeyman will get you." I can remember telling him I wasn't afraid of the bogeyman because I slept on the second floor, and he couldn't get in my room. He said, "Oh, but the bogeyman is twenty feet tall and he can look into your window." He told me it didn't matter how safe you were, he was *there*. I remember that night being awake, worried about the bogeyman.

Quoted in Joseph McBride, *Steven Spielberg: A Biography*. Jackson: University Press of Mississippi, 2010, p. 59.

*E.T.* replaces the spectacular visual effects of *Close Encounters* with an emphasis on human—and alien—emotions. Of all of his sci-fi films, *E.T.* is Spielberg's most personal one. He relates in an interview that he "wanted to tell the story of the divorce of my parents. Elliott's not me, but yes, he's the closest thing to my experience in life, growing up in suburbia."[9] Spielberg's directing style accentuated the childlike theme of the movie. He used low camera angles to emphasize the children's perspective of events, and many of the adult characters were shown only from the waist down.

*E.T.* was another blockbuster for Spielberg, and it became even more of a cultural phenomenon than *Close Encounters*, flooding the marketplace with toys, books, E.T. dolls, and movie-related apparel. The catchphrase "E.T. phone home" (E.T.'s expression of his longing to reconnect with his own kind) was heard everywhere. For Spielberg, *E.T. the Extra-Terrestrial* became a turning point. Years of making movies about aliens and UFOs, had caused some critics to question his ability to make serious films but Spielberg was ready to move forward. *E.T.* marked "the end of my childhood," he recalls, "and it gave me the courage . . . to start to tackle more adult subjects."[10] Many of Spielberg's later films examined significant social and historical topics—and won critical praise. These included *Amistad*, which focused on slavery; *Schindler's List*, which focused on the Holocaust; and *Lincoln*, which examined the last four months of Abraham Lincoln's life.

## The Spielberg Legacy

Spielberg did not abandon science fiction, however. He explored the idea of man's abuse of science (as author Mary Shelley did in *Frankenstein*) in 1993's *Jurassic Park* and its 1997 sequel, *The Lost World: Jurassic Park*. In these films, cloned dinosaurs created for a theme park go on deadly rampages. In 2001's *A.I. Artificial Intelligence*, a robotic boy must come to terms with the human emotions his creators have given him. The next year Spielberg's *Minority Report* revealed the dark side of crime and punishment in the future. In 2005 he reimagined H.G. Wells's alien invasion story, *War of the Worlds*.

> "[*E.T. the Extra-Terrestrial* marked] the end of my childhood, and it gave me the courage . . . to start to tackle more adult subjects."[10]
>
> —*Steven Spielberg*

Steven Spielberg turned seventy years old in 2016, but retirement seemed to be far from his thoughts. Future projects for the director include *Ready Player One*, a film based on a popular science fiction novel by Ernest Cline; a new entry in the Indiana Jones series; a film based on Roald Dahl's 1982 children's book about a giant entitled *The BFG;* and a sequel to the 2015 dinosaur blockbuster *Jurassic World*. If his past successes in science fiction cinema are any indication, moviegoers will continue to thrill to Spielberg's unique vision of what the world may become in a future they can only imagine.

# CHAPTER 2

# George Lucas

From the look of the crumpled remains of the sports car sitting under the tree it had just uprooted in a violent crash, it seemed impossible that the occupant could have survived. A speeding Chevy Impala had smashed into the side of the small Fiat, snapping the driver's seat belt and throwing him clear of the wreck. Although hospitalized in serious condition, the driver eventually recovered.

That accident, which occurred on a sweltering afternoon in June 1962, was a turning point for the Fiat's driver, eighteen-year-old George Lucas. Before his brush with death, he spent most of his time driving around Modesto, California, doing just enough schoolwork to get by. While recovering in the hospital, Lucas says he "decided to go straight, to be a better student, to try to do something with myself."[11] That "something" eventually became one of the most successful movie franchises of all time.

## Growing Up in Modesto

Modesto was a quiet northern California town surrounded by farmland when George Walton Lucas Jr. was born there on May 14, 1944. The third child in a family of four children, George was the only boy and the one his father hoped would eventually run the family stationery store. George's mother, Dorothy, was in frail health but took on the role of homemaker for the growing Lucas brood with the help of a housekeeper.

George had an active imagination, fueled by his love of comic books and by the rapidly growing new medium of television. When his father brought home a brand new black-and-white television set in 1954, George was hooked. He devoured whatever came across the flickering tube, from westerns and cartoons to old films. George was especially drawn to adventure serial movies that had been popular in theaters during the 1930s and 1940s. Serials told a continuing story by showing one episode a week. Each episode ended in a cliffhanger, which left the hero in peril and kept audiences coming back week after week. One such serial, the sci-fi classic *Flash Gordon Conquers the Universe*, would have an impact on George's later interest in science fiction cinema.

## California Cruising

As Lucas entered adolescence, his life revolved around cars: fixing them, racing them, and cruising the streets of Modesto. He was only a few days away from his high school graduation when his near-fatal accident changed everything. Fully recovered by the fall of 1962, Lucas began classes at Modesto Junior College. His grades were a marked improvement over his high school record, and he graduated in 1964. His father hoped his son would now join him in the family business. But young Lucas had other plans. In junior college he discovered he had a talent for filming with an eight-millimeter camera his father had given him. Shy and self-conscious, he felt comfortable behind the camera. "Lucas discovered the pleasures of watching," observes film critic John Baxter, "ideally through the lens of a camera. People didn't ask awkward questions when you filmed them; they just let you be."[12]

> "Lucas discovered the pleasures of watching, ideally through the lens of a camera. People didn't ask awkward questions when you filmed them; they just let you be."[12]
>
> —Film critic John Baxter

*As an adolescent in the 1950s, George Lucas was interested in the adventure tales he read in comics and saw on television. His interest in old movie serials, such as the Flash Gordon stories that were rebroadcast on TV, would influence the characters and narrative structure of* Star Wars.

After junior college Lucas enrolled in the film program at the University of Southern California (USC) in Los Angeles. Lucas's father ridiculed his son's decision to pursue a film career. "You're never going to get a real job," the elder Lucas shouted. "You'll be back in a few years." To this, George snapped, "I'm never coming back! I'm going to be a millionaire before I'm thirty."[13] With those words, Lucas packed up and headed to Los Angeles.

# Film School

At USC, Lucas found himself surrounded by other students who shared his passion for filmmaking. Many would, like Lucas, go on to build successful careers in Hollywood. Lucas's first film at USC, a one-minute animation entitled *Look at Life*, was a montage of photos that appeared in *Life* magazine. Other student productions followed as Lucas refined his skills, including *1:42:08*, a film about one of his favorite subjects—a racing car.

After graduating with a bachelor's degree in 1966, Lucas was eager to start his career. He got a job as an assistant to veteran film editor Verna Fields, who was editing films for the US government. While working with Fields, Lucas met another young editor named Marcia Griffin, whom he married in 1969. After adopting a daughter, the two eventually split, divorcing in 1983. Lucas remained a single father, adopting two more children, before marrying Mellody Hobson in 2013.

By the late 1960s science fiction was beginning to appear once more in the popular media, as demonstrated by the television series *Star Trek*. Lucas's first entry into the sci-fi genre would be a student film.

# A Dystopian Future

Lucas returned to USC as a graduate student in 1967. There he wrote and directed *THX 1138:4EB*, a fifteen-minute film telling the story of a man struggling to escape government oppression in a bleak futuristic world. The film won first prize in the 1968 National Student Film Festival and received critical praise. "*THX* was an astonishing piece of student work," writes critic Charles Champlin. "It was obvious that Lucas was someone to watch."[14]

Lucas wanted to make a feature-length version of *THX 1138:4EB*, and Warner Brothers agreed to fund and distribute the project. With a budget of under $1 million, which was small compared to other Hollywood films of the time, Lucas filmed the movie in and around San Francisco in his own creative manner. "I'm very documentary in style," he explains, "just set up all the cameras and shoot the scene."[15]

When the finished film, now called simply *THX 1138*, was shown to Warner Brothers in 1970, studio executives hated it. They disliked the film's stark visuals and lack of a clear plot, and they declared that it needed reediting. The studio's new version, which cut only four minutes from the film, was a failure at the box office. Lucas was furious that such a personal project had been taken away from him, and he denounced Warner Brothers: "Making film is an art," he said. "Selling film is a business. The trouble is they [Warner Brothers] don't know how to sell films."[16]

Although disillusioned with the studio's handling of *THX*, Lucas was not finished with science fiction. After his next project, a film about small-town cruising called *American Graffiti*, became a huge hit (and one of the most profitable films of all time), Lucas's talent as a director was finally established. He could now make whatever films he wanted.

> "Making film is an art. Selling film is a business."[16]
>
> —George Lucas

## The Origin of Star Wars

The question for Lucas was, what should his next film be? He had never forgotten the thrill of watching *Flash Gordon Conquers the Universe* on television. After unsuccessfully trying to purchase the rights to remake the Flash Gordon serials, he decided to re-create that thrill within a universe of his own making. Lucas began studying fantasy, fairy tales, and other subjects that he might use as the basis of his own sci-fi mythology. Religion played a part in forming a major aspect of Lucas's film. He explains that "the 'Force of others' is what all basic religions are based on, especially the eastern religions."[17] In *Star Wars*, the Force would become the underlying theme that propelled the action.

In May 1973 Lucas made a deal with Twentieth Century Fox to write and direct his sci-fi epic. After spending the next three years writing four script drafts, Lucas was ready to film *Star Wars*.

## A Galaxy Far, Far Away

After the rigors of shooting on location for both *THX 1138* and *American Graffiti*, Lucas was eager to direct *Star Wars*, which

# Skywalker Ranch

Nestled in the lush countryside of Marin County, California, is a ranch like no other on earth. Instead of herds of cattle or horses, the products of Skywalker Ranch appear on countless movie screens and entertain millions of fans worldwide. George Lucas designed Skywalker Ranch to provide a creative atmosphere where he and like-minded independent filmmakers could make movies without having to deal with the Hollywood establishment. With his share of profits from *The Empire Strikes Back*, Lucas purchased an old cattle ranch located about 30 miles (48 km) north of San Francisco. What he eventually built there is a nearly 5,000 acre (2,023 ha) community dedicated to making cinematic dreams.

The Technical Building houses the latest in filmmaking technology: thirty-four editing suites, six audio mixing studios, a stage for scoring productions, and a three-hundred-seat screening theater. The Main House is a Victorian-style mansion that houses meeting rooms and Lucas's office. The most impressive room in the Main House is the Lucasfilm Research Library. Under a stained-glass dome, the two-story library contains thousands of resources for producers, directors, costume designers, and other production personnel. An inn provides twenty-six rooms for clients to reside in while working at Skywalker Ranch.

The ranch has its own farm, with vineyards, organic gardens, bee colonies, and an olive grove, which produce wine, honey, and organic vegetables for purchase in the ranch's General Store. There is even a fully manned Skywalker Ranch Fire Department to protect the estate.

was mainly a studio-based film. But first, some exterior sequences needed to be filmed. The deserts of Tunisia in northern Africa represented the planet Tatooine, and Lucas brought his crew there in March 1976. Immediately, everything went wrong. The desert, which had had no rain for years, was drenched by a four-day downpour. Sandstorms pitted the camera lenses and forced the crew to wear protective goggles. The little droid R2-D2, one of several robots built specially for the movie, kept falling over during takes. After a grueling two weeks, Lucas finally got the shots he needed, so he moved his crew to Elstree Studios in England.

Filming went better at Elstree, but it was not problem-free. Illness among the crew and actors, strict British union rules, and a brutal heat wave disrupted filming and led to discord on the set.

Lucas's style of directing did not help matters. Lucas has been described by those who have worked with him as someone who is not comfortable directing actors or building rapport with them. Nor does he like to concern himself with a character's motivation. "I have a sneaking suspicion," comments Mark Hamill, who played Luke Skywalker, "that if there were a way to make movies without actors, George would do it."[18] At Elstree, much of Lucas's direction consisted of curt phrases such as "Do it again, only better" and "Faster and more intense."[19] He counted heavily on his cast to instinctively know what to do during their scenes.

While Lucas was directing his actors, his mind was occupied with the visual aspects of his film. He knew that the special effects would make or break the movie.

> "I have a sneaking suspicion that if there were a way to make movies without actors, George would do it."[18]
>
> —Actor Mark Hamill

## Dogfights in Space

Like the World War II aerial dogfights he had seen on television, Lucas wanted his film to soar with scenes of dueling spaceships. "I'd never seen a space battle," Lucas says. "I'd seen flying around in serials like *Flash Gordon*, but they were really dopey. . . . I wanted to see this incredible aerial ballet in outer space."[20] There was just one problem: the technology for creating his aerial ballet did not exist. In 1975 Lucas formed a new company called Industrial Light and Magic (ILM) to create the visual effects for *Star Wars*. To head up the project, Lucas hired veteran special effects master John Dykstra.

As ILM's chief designer, Dykstra invented a computer-controlled camera that could twist, turn, and swoop around model spaceships to simulate the movements of a dogfight in space. Lucas now had the means to create his vision, but getting that vision on film was a formidable task. The script called for some 360 individual special effects shots, more than had been created for any previous film. Once, when Lucas visited ILM to

*George Lucas accepted a low salary for directing* Star Wars, *but he kept the merchandising rights and the rights to the sequels. Little did movie executives suspect the films and characters (such as Jedi Master Yoda, left) would be so beloved that Lucas's fortune was ensured through toy and product licensing.*

check on its progress, he was appalled by what he learned: of the 360 special effects shots, only three were finished.

## Launching Star Wars

*Star Wars* was over budget and behind schedule. Lucas began supervising the production of the special effects. Sets were being built and filmed almost before the paint was dry. By the last few weeks of production, Lucas had several crews filming simultaneously in order to get the final shots. After filming was completed, final editing, integrating the special effects footage, and the sound mix all had to be done. The release of *Star Wars* was set for May 25, 1977, and Lucas rushed to meet the deadline. He hoped that his film might make as much as a typical Disney movie, about $16 million. It was an underestimate of galactic proportions.

On May 25, Lucas and his wife were eating at a restaurant across the street from the famous Mann's Chinese Theatre in Hollywood. Looking out the window, Lucas saw huge crowds of people

# Lucas on Directing

When filming on location, a director's life is filled with intense pressure, numerous problems that crop up at the worst possible moments, and very little sleep. Lucas describes what his typical day was like while making *Star Wars:*

> When you're directing, you have to get up at four thirty [in the morning], have breakfast at five, leave the hotel at six, drive an hour to location, start shooting at eight, and finish shooting around six. Then you wrap, go to your office, and set up the next day's work. You get back to the hotel about eight or nine, hopefully get a bite to eat, then you go to your room and figure out your homework, how you're going to shoot the next day's scenes, and then you go to sleep. The next morning it starts all over again.

Quoted in Dale Pollock, *Skywalking: The Life and Films of George Lucas.* New York: Harmony, 1983, p. 159.

lining up in front of the theater. He was stunned when he looked at the marquee: the crowd was there to see *Star Wars*. Unknown to Lucas, his movie had replaced the film originally scheduled for that night. "I don't believe this," Lucas recalls saying. "It wasn't excitement, it was amazement. I felt it was some kind of aberration."[21]

But it was no fluke. *Star Wars* became a worldwide phenomenon, eventually earning $441 million at the box office (over $1 billion in today's dollars). Soon stores were filled with all manner of *Star Wars* merchandise, which became a windfall for Lucas. In his original contract with Twentieth Century Fox, Lucas had agreed to write and direct *Star Wars* for $150,000. But he shrewdly retained the rights to *Star Wars* merchandise as well as control over any sequels. At the time, these rights seemed insignificant to Twentieth Century Fox executives, who saw *Star Wars* as just another little movie unlikely to become a major hit. The studio's deal made Lucas richer and more powerful than anyone had imagined possible.

## Star Wars and the Lucas Legacy

*Star Wars* was a hit, but Lucas was not finished with his outer space saga. "It wasn't long after I began writing *Star Wars*," Lucas later commented, "that I realized the story was more than a single film could hold. . . . I began to see it as a tale that could take at least nine films to tell—three trilogies."[22] *Star Wars* (renamed *Star Wars Episode IV: A New Hope* upon its rerelease in 1981) was the first film in the middle trilogy. Two more *Star Wars* films completed the trilogy: *Episode V: The Empire Strikes Back* in 1980 and *Episode VI: Return of the Jedi* in 1983. Both new films were tremendous successes, but Lucas did not direct either of them. In fact, he would not get behind the camera for another twenty years, concentrating instead on writing and producing films, including *Raiders of the Lost Ark* and its sequels. He returned to directing in 1997 to make the three films composing the first *Star Wars* trilogy, which provided the backstory for the original film.

Lucas's legacy reaches beyond the realm of science fiction. With a fortune of more than $5 billion (much of it from the 2012 sale of his company Lucasfilm to Disney), Lucas tops the list of Hollywood's richest filmmakers. He has pledged to donate one half of his wealth to charitable causes. Lucas supports such varied organizations as the Make-A-Wish Foundation for critically ill children; the Jackie Robinson Foundation, which provides college scholarships for minority students; and Stand Up To Cancer, to fund cancer research.

The George Lucas Educational Foundation, established in 1991, works with schools to develop programs that help students succeed. In 2014, Lucas chose Chicago as the future home of the Lucas Museum of Narrative Arts, which will celebrate the power of images and how they affect the world. The museum is scheduled to open in 2018.

> "I'd never seen a space battle. I'd seen flying around in serials like Flash Gordon, but they were really dopey. . . . I wanted to see this incredible aerial ballet in outer space."[20]
>
> —George Lucas

Despite the unprecedented success of the *Star Wars* saga, Lucas never won an Academy Award for directing. The young man who was so infatuated with Flash Gordon went on to create films of such spectacular vision and adventure that they became cultural touchstones for generations of fans worldwide.

# CHAPTER 3

# Stanley Kubrick

**B**y the spring of 1964, the space race between the United States and the Soviet Union was in full swing. President John F. Kennedy had declared in 1961 that the United States would put a man on the moon by the end of the decade, and the National Aeronautics and Space Administration (NASA) was working feverishly to accomplish that goal. NASA had ended the Mercury space program and was gearing up for its next phase in space exploration, the two-man Gemini program. The Soviet Union was also making progress, including sending the first woman into space.

In April 1964 two men met at a restaurant called Trader Vic's in New York City. The men were neither scientists nor astronauts: one was a writer, the other a film director. Their meeting would result in a collaboration that changed the way the world thought of outer space. The writer, a British author named Arthur C. Clarke, described the vision held by the man who shared his table: "He wanted to make a movie about man's place in the universe—a project likely to give a heart attack to any studio head."[23] The man sitting across from Clarke was a fiercely independent film director not inclined to worry too much about the health of a movie company executive. If anyone could accomplish such a formidable task, it was Stanley Kubrick.

## A New York Childhood

The Bronx, one of the five boroughs of New York City, was a growing middle-class neighborhood populated with Italian, Irish, and Jewish immigrants after World War I. It was here that physician Jacques Kubrick settled in 1927 with his wife, Gertrude. Stanley, their first child, was born on July 26, 1928. Kubrick's early grammar school education, which began in 1934, was marked by a dismal attendance record: school did not interest Kubrick, and in his first two terms he was absent as much as he was present. His social skills were also less than satisfactory, and he often received poor marks in such areas as having respect for others and playing well with his schoolmates. A year of attending school in California while living with his uncle did not increase his interest in academics. "I never learned anything at school," he once declared, "and I never read a book for pleasure until I was 19."[24]

> "[Kubrick] wanted to make a movie about man's place in the universe—a project likely to give a heart attack to any studio head."[23]
>
> —Author Arthur C. Clarke

Away from school, one of Kubrick's interests was chess. Taught the game by his father in an attempt to stimulate his son's intellect, Kubrick became an avid player. He later explained how chess impacted his directing career. "If chess has any relation to filmmaking," he said, "it would be in the way it helps you develop patience and discipline in choosing between alternatives at a time when an impulsive decision seems very attractive."[25]

## Kubrick's First Camera

In 1941 Kubrick's father gave him a Graflex camera for his thirteenth birthday. Kubrick quickly learned how to use it and began photographing people on the streets of the Bronx. In the days before digital photography, cameras took pictures on negatives that had to be chemically developed and printed in total darkness. A friend of Kubrick's had built a darkroom to process his own photographs. Kubrick spent many hours there, watching his pictures appear, as if by magic, in the trays of developing fluid. As a student at William Howard Taft High School, Kubrick became a photographer for the school newspaper. Herman Getter, an art teacher at Taft, observed a spark of creativity in Kubrick's photographs. "I saw in him," Getter recalls, "a certain eagerness, a certain feeling for the use of the camera as an art medium."[26]

Kubrick also spent hours at local movie theaters, watching the latest Hollywood features. He was disappointed by what he saw on the screen. "I didn't know anything about making films," he recalls, "but I believed that I couldn't make them any worse than the majority of films I was seeing. Bad films gave me the courage to try making a movie."[27] Although filmmaking was still in his future, Kubrick's creativity in still photography soon made an impression with a national magazine.

> "I didn't know anything about making films, but I believed that I couldn't make them any worse than the majority of films I was seeing. Bad films gave me the courage to try making a movie."[27]
>
> —*Stanley Kubrick*

## The World Through a Lens

In an age before television, people read magazines to keep in touch with the world. *Life* magazine and its competitor, *Look*, brought news and entertainment features into America's homes using words and photographs. In 1945 Kubrick took a poignant photograph of a newspaper seller's reaction to the death of President Franklin D. Roosevelt. In a bold move, Kubrick showed the picture to *Look*'s photo editor, who paid him twenty-five dollars to run it in the magazine. Not long after, he was hired as a staff photographer for the magazine. At seventeen years old, Kubrick was now a professional photographer.

In the five years that Kubrick worked for *Look*, he shot numerous photo-essays, including "Prizefighter," published on January

*Stanley Kubrick worked in collaboration with novelist Arthur C. Clarke to bring to life the cinematic masterpiece* 2001: A Space Odyssey. *In the film, which Kubrick directed, astronauts make contact with an alien artifact that seems to hold secrets of humanity's place in the universe.*

18, 1949. His eighteen black-and-white photographs captured boxer Walter Cartier relaxing, getting ready for a fight, and boxing in the ring. When Kubrick decided to make a film in 1950, he chose Cartier as his subject. With money saved from his job at *Look*, Kubrick made a short documentary called *Day of the Fight*. It follows Cartier preparing for a bout against opponent Bobby James and ultimately winning the fight by a knockout. Kubrick sold *Day of the Fight* for $4,000, making a $100 profit. Two more documentaries followed, as well as Kubrick's first dramatic film, a war movie entitled *Fear and Desire*.

While Kubrick's professional life was on an upswing, his personal life produced two failed marriages. In 1948 Kubrick had married Toba Metz, his high school sweetheart. Divorced in 1951, Kubrick then married dancer Ruth Sobatka, a union that ended after only five years. His next marriage, to German actress Christiane Harlan, lasted forty years, until Kubrick's death in 1999. The couple moved to England in 1961, making it their permanent home and Kubrick's filmmaking headquarters. Although Kubrick had earned a pilot's license in 1947, he had an intense fear of flying. This, plus the fact that he seldom left England or gave interviews, led some to call him a recluse. But Kubrick simply felt that England had the best studios for the films he wanted to make.

By the mid-1960s Kubrick had directed numerous films, including the highly successful historical epic *Spartacus* and *Dr. Strangelove or: How I Learned to Stop Worrying and Love the Bomb*, a comedic satire on the foibles of humans trying to cope with the danger of nuclear war. For his next film, Kubrick decided to enter the world of science fiction.

## A Journey Beyond the Stars

One of the influences on Kubrick's science fiction masterpiece *2001: A Space Odyssey* was a 1948 short story by Arthur C. Clarke. In Clarke's "The Sentinel," an alien artifact left on the moon millions of years ago is discovered by human lunar explorers. It is a beacon to the aliens, and it signals that humanity has finally achieved the ability to leave Earth and begin exploring the universe.

Movies are often produced from novels, but for *2001* the process was reversed. Clarke recalls that he and Kubrick "let our imaginations soar freely by writing a complete novel, from which we would later derive the script."[28] The novel was completed in December 1964, and Kubrick made a deal with MGM to make the film, which was originally called *Journey Beyond the Stars*. The story of the film, and the novel, spans the prehistoric world of humanity's simian ancestors to a future of space travel and alien encounters. The film opens with a group of prehuman apes. Thanks to a mysterious black slab called a monolith, they learn to use bones as weapons. It then flashes forward to the year 2001, when another monolith is found buried on the moon. Upon its discovery, the monolith sends a signal to Jupiter, prompting scientists to embark on a voyage to that planet to discover the slab's purpose. In contrast to the low-budget

# Kubrick as Auteur

To make a film, hundreds of people are needed to write the script, design makeup and costumes, light the sets, and operate the cameras and microphones. And yet one person is the engine that makes the whole filmmaking machine go: the director. The auteur theory (the word *auteur* is French for "author") states that the director uses his or her medium for self-expression and makes sure every aspect of the production follows his or her personal vision. William Reed Woodfield, a photographer on Kubrick's film *Spartacus*, recounts Kubrick's early job as a photographer as leading to his auteur status:

> When you're a seventeen-year-old photographer on the staff of *Look* magazine and you go out and do a story, you are in total control of that story. What you frame, what you take, the mood you take it in, the pictures you mark for printing, what you turn in—you are in complete control. And it is a wonderful feeling.

Other famous auteurs in cinema are suspense master Alfred Hitchcock; the director of the classic *Citizen Kane*, Orson Welles; and western director John Ford. Each director stamped his own personality on his films. As for Kubrick, from his early prizefight documentaries to *2001: A Space Odyssey*, his artistic hand is evident in each frame of his films.

Quoted in John Baxter, *Stanley Kubrick: A Biography*. New York: Carroll & Graf, 1997, p. 30.

sci-fi movies of the time, Kubrick's film would not feature flying saucers attacking Earth with death rays or pretty girls screaming while being abducted by fake-looking aliens. Instead of using black-and-white film, the standard for sci-fi B movies, Kubrick's budget of $10.5 million allowed him to film in color using a newly developed wide-screen process called Cinerama. Kubrick chose to make *2001* for the eye rather than the ear. Of the film's 140-minute running time, only 40 minutes contain dialogue. "I tried to create a visual experience," Kubrick later commented, "one that . . . directly penetrates the subconscious with an emotional and philosophic content."[29]

Kubrick conducted extensive research to make sure *2001* would be as authentic as possible. Science journalist Piers Bizony writes that "Kubrick wanted absolute realism: he wanted the

*Kubrick's vision of space accentuated its remoteness and its unfamiliarity. To reflect this in the human-inhabited space stations and craft, he utilized uncluttered, predominantly white, modernist sets that felt futuristic yet sterile.*

hardware on screen to look as though it really *worked*."[30] Ever the perfectionist, Kubrick went to extremes to obtain authenticity. Once, when Clarke casually mentioned that a spaceship flight deck set did not look quite right, Kubrick had the entire thing ripped out and redesigned. More than one hundred model makers were employed to create the most authentic spaceships ever recorded on film to that time. Some of those models were still being constructed as Kubrick began production on *2001*.

## Picturing the Future

Kubrick filmed *2001* in England, beginning on December 29, 1965, at two studios large enough to handle sets as diverse as an excavation site on the moon, an African savanna, and the interior of the fictional spaceship *Discovery*. One of the most talked-about sets, the living quarters of the *Discovery* was a huge drum some 40 feet (12 m) in diameter and 10 feet (3 m) wide. Built for Kubrick by an aircraft manufacturer at a cost of $750,000, the drum revolved like a Ferris wheel: in the film, such rotation provides artificial gravity for the astronauts.

Kubrick coordinated the production from a trailer that served as his command post. John Baxter, author of a Kubrick biography, notes, "He sees the set as a battlefield and himself as its general. Establishing control of a production and the people on it is integral to his method."[31] Despite conflicts with the British crew, there was little discord during the production. "This is a happy set," commented Keir Dullea, who played astronaut Dave Bowman, "and that's something."[32] Kubrick's skill in using visuals to tell a story is evident in the completed film. Early in the movie, an ape tosses his newly acquired weapon, a bone, into the air. At the height of its trajectory, Kubrick abruptly cuts to a nuclear bomb orbiting Earth, matching the flight of the ape's weapon. In one simple cut, Kubrick has summarized the evolution of human weaponry and advanced the story by 4 million years.

> "[Kubrick] sees the set as a battlefield and himself as its general. Establishing control of a production and the people on it is integral to his method."[31]
>
> —Author John Baxter

The most spectacular scene comes near the end of the film, when Bowman is transported through space and time in a colorful, mind-expanding rush of light and visual sensation in what is called the Star Gate sequence. Kubrick desired something fantastic and told Doug Trumbull, his supervisor of special effects, that he wanted the camera to seem to "go through something."[33] As computer-generated images had not yet been invented, Trumbull modified a process known as slit-scan photography to create Bowman's seemingly endless flight through infinite space. In the finished film, the Star Gate sequence is so intense that many people became dizzy or even ill just from watching it.

It took about two and a half years to create all 205 special effect scenes in *2001*. When critics finally viewed Kubrick's

# Kubrick's Last Sci-fi Film

A 1969 short story by British science fiction writer Brian Aldiss was the inspiration for a film that Kubrick hoped to make but never did. Aldiss's story centers around a robot boy and the struggles of his human mother to bond with her child. Kubrick read the story, entitled "Supertoys Last All Summer Long," and thought he could make it into a film.

Kubrick worked on the project with Aldiss and other writers throughout the 1980s and 1990s, but the story, now called *A.I.* (for *Artificial Intelligence*), never came together. Kubrick also felt that the current state of computer graphics was not sophisticated enough for *A.I.* Other film projects took up his time, and *A.I.* remained stalled. Then, on March 7, 1999, Kubrick died. Fortunately, Steven Spielberg was there to carry on the work of making *A.I.* real. Kubrick had been in conversation with Spielberg about the film since 1985 and had even asked him to direct, which Spielberg declined. Now Spielberg took Kubrick's notes and ninety-page treatment and wrote the script for the film, renamed *A.I. Artificial Intelligence*. As director, Spielberg was mindful of the project's originator. "I did a lot of Stanley's shots," Spielberg recalls. "I wanted to get as much of what Stanley wanted upon the screen as I possibly could." When *A.I. Artificial Intelligence* opened in theaters in 2001, moviegoers could finally enjoy Kubrick's last sci-fi film.

Quoted in Rachel Abramowitz, "Regarding Stanley," *Los Angeles Times*, May 6, 2001. www.latimes.com.

masterpiece, the excellence of its special effects was about the only thing they agreed on.

## Legacy

*2001: A Space Odyssey* premiered on April 4, 1968, to mixed reviews. Some critics did not know what to think of a film that dazzled the eye but had so little dialogue as to make it almost impossible to understand. Renata Adler of the *New York Times* wrote, "The movie is so completely absorbed in its own problems . . . that it is somewhere between hypnotic and immensely boring."[34] But audiences, especially younger moviegoers looking to get a "high" from the Star Gate sequence, were generally enthusiastic. By 1972, *2001* had grossed $31 million worldwide. Today it is considered a classic of science fiction cinema.

When Kubrick died on March 7, 1999, his passing was mourned by science fiction and film fans around the world. Clarke lamented the fact that his friend and collaborator did not live to see 2001, the year Kubrick had made so famous in popular culture. His unfinished projects include a biographical film about Napoléon Bonaparte, for which he did extensive research and wrote a screenplay, and several ideas for films set in World War II.

Today space travel has not yet lived up to Kubrick's vision of orbiting hotels and voyages to Jupiter. But his influence on such celebrated directors as George Lucas, James Cameron, and Christopher Nolan assure his place in the universe of cinema's science fiction stars.

# CHAPTER 4

# James Cameron

**D**uring the 1960s a daring experiment was carried out in Canada's Chippawa Creek. A brave diver was placed inside a bathysphere, a vessel designed to explore underwater environments. It slowly descended to the bottom of the creek and, after a few minutes, returned to the surface. The experiment was deemed a success by its creator, a young boy named James Cameron. The bathysphere actually was a jar placed in a bucket that he had lowered into the river. The heroic but somewhat unwilling diver—a mouse—suffered no ill effects from his journey.

This simple experiment reveals the keen sense of curiosity, the knack for building gadgets, and the interest in exploration that were second nature for the future filmmaker. As the director of numerous blockbuster science fiction movies, Cameron explored on film not only the inner space of the oceans but the outer space of his own mind's creation.

## A Canadian Boyhood

James Cameron was born on August 16, 1954, to parents Philip and Shirley in Kapuskasing, Ontario. When James was five years old, his family moved to the Niagara Falls area, eventually settling into the quiet community of Chippawa. As the oldest in a family of five children, James became the natural leader of his younger siblings. One of his strengths, even at an early age, was the ability to organize people to get things done. Weekends and summers would find him with his friends building things from all kinds of found materials.

Encouraged by his artist mother, Cameron showed an early interest in drawing. "Everything I liked and reacted to," he recalls, "I immediately had to draw. Drawing was my way of owning it."[35] He sketched ancient artifacts at the Royal Ontario Museum in Toronto, and he created his own comic books based on fantasy and science fiction films. Cameron avidly read the works of popular science fiction authors. "I was an absolutely rabid science fiction fan," he recalls. "When I read science fiction I saw stuff in my head that I had never seen in films."[36]

One film that had a major impact on his career was Stanley Kubrick's science fiction masterpiece *2001: A Space Odyssey*. Fourteen-year-old Cameron was fascinated by the incredible visuals of the film, especially one sequence, a dazzling kaleidoscopic trip through space. "It had such an effect on me that I was physically ill," he recalls. "I also wanted to find out how it was done, so I started studying photography and special effects."[37] Using a borrowed Super 8 camera, Cameron and a friend began making short sci-fi movies featuring model spaceships they had built.

> "I was an absolutely rabid science fiction fan. When I read science fiction I saw stuff in my head that I had never seen in films."[36]
>
> —*James Cameron*

## Searching for a Career

In 1971 Philip Cameron's job took his family to Brea, California, a suburb of Los Angeles. James enrolled at Fullerton College but, not finding courses that interested him, he eventually dropped out. His interest in filmmaking remained, however. On weekends he went to the library at the University of Southern California and taught himself the art of film special effects by reading everything he could find on the subject.

*James Cameron (left) on the set of* Avatar *with actor Sam Worthington. Cameron has always been interested in the marriage of special effects and moviemaking.* Avatar *allowed him to use CGI to create a fully realized world on-screen with which his human actors could interact.*

When *Star Wars* became a blockbuster hit in 1977, Cameron and a group of friends decided to make their own sci-fi movie. Cameron directed the twelve-minute film, titled *Xenogenesis*; his friends played the film's characters. But the real stars of the short movie were the visual effects. With models animated by stop-motion photography, laser cannon explosions, and composited sequences (where several shots are combined to create a single image), *Xenogenesis* proved that Cameron's self-education in special effects had paid off.

## The Rise of *The Terminator*

In Hollywood, a B-movie director named Roger Corman was preparing a space epic entitled *Battle Beyond the Stars*. Corman saw

*Xenogenesis* and immediately hired Cameron as a model maker. Working day and night on the film's spaceships, Cameron was soon promoted to art director, supervising the look of the entire film.

In 1982 an Italian producer hired Cameron to direct a movie called *Piranha II: The Spawning*. It was his first real job as a director, but a few weeks after filming began in Jamaica, Cameron was fired. Traveling to Italy to confront the producer, Cameron learned that this had been the plan all along. To comply with the distributor's requirement that an American director be credited for the film, the producer hired Cameron to shoot some scenes and then dismissed him, finishing the film himself. Thus Cameron's name could legally appear in the credits, although he never considered himself the director of *Piranha II*. While in Rome, Cameron fell ill with a raging fever. One night during his illness he dreamed of "a metallic death figure rising Phoenix-like out of fire."[38] It was the genesis of the apocalyptic sci-fi film *The Terminator*, which catapulted Cameron into the ranks of Hollywood's elite young directors.

When Cameron awoke from his fevered dream, he sketched the figure he had dreamed about. Upon his return to California, Cameron and a friend penned a script about the figure: a cyborg assassin from the future—a Terminator—sent back in time to kill an innocent woman. The theme of machines rebelling against their makers was then a popular one in sci-fi movies.

> "Personally, I only feel comfortable with women I can respect, that can hold their own, that have some kind of strength of character. And I think that translates into the women I write for films."[39]
>
> —*James Cameron*

For the Terminator role, Cameron cast Arnold Schwarzenegger, a world-class bodybuilder who had acted in several forgettable films. For the film's female lead, a relatively unknown actress named Linda Hamilton was chosen. Her character, Sarah Connor, was the first in a series of strong-willed women who populated Cameron's films. "Personally," Cameron says, "I only feel comfortable with women I can respect, that can hold their own, that have some kind of strength of character. And I think that translates into the women I write for films."[39] Cameron collaborated with special effects veteran Stan Winston on the design of the Terminator, which ended up almost identical to Cameron's fever-induced vision.

## Directing *The Terminator*

Cameron's take-charge method of directing was in full display on *The Terminator* set. Schwarzenegger recalls that "if a shot was a half an inch off from the way he visualized it, he would go crazy."[40] Schwarzenegger's costar Hamilton agrees: "Jim was a total taskmaster. . . . He didn't make a lot of room to satisfy his actors."[41] If Cameron was a taskmaster, he was also a fearless director. Rather than simply describing a stunt, he would demonstrate it, as Schwarzenegger remembers: "He jumped on this Honda motorcycle I was supposed to be riding and accelerated and spun around, did a one-eighty to show me what he wanted. I thought he was crazy."[42]

> "[Cameron] jumped on this Honda motorcycle I was supposed to be riding and accelerated and spun around, did a one-eighty to show me what he wanted. I thought he was crazy."[42]
>
> —*Actor Arnold Schwarzenegger*

After Cameron completed *The Terminator*, he learned that Orion, the studio releasing the film, had little confidence in his vision of the future. Studio executives thought the film would play in theaters for a few weeks and then disappear. When *The Terminator* opened in October 1984, its reception proved Orion wrong. Audiences cheered and critics raved. *Variety*, the Hollywood trade magazine, called it a "blazing cinematic comic book full of virtuoso filmmaking, solid performances, and a compelling story."[43] The film took in $77 million worldwide at the box office.

*The Terminator* became a science fiction classic and made a star of Arnold Schwarzenegger. For Cameron, it was a source of personal pride. "This movie has the things in it I wanted to see in a movie when I was sixteen. It has robots, pretty girls, time travel, and action."[44] His next film would add terrifying aliens to his list.

# Creating a New Reality

Since actors are not 10-foot-tall (3 m) blue creatures, makeup and costuming could not provide the realism that *Avatar* required. Thus, Cameron had to create the Na'vi race using a technique called performance capture. Rather than donning costumes and acting on real sets, the actors wore form-fitting black suits studded with reflective markers. As they performed in a vast, empty warehouse called the Volume, dozens of cameras recorded infrared reflections from the markers and sent the information to computers. There, CGI programs turned the human actors into the Na'vi within the virtual world of Pandora. Using a special system called Simulcam, Cameron could see the live action as it took place against the computer-generated backgrounds, watching his alien world come to life.

Although the actors' body movements were relatively easy to capture, their facial expressions, essential for creating believable beings, were more difficult. Cameron came up with a system using blue dots applied to an actor's face. The performer put on a head-worn rig that had a miniature boom-mounted camera pointing directly at his or her face. Computers translated the motion of the dots, which followed the actors' expressions, into digital information that CGI artists used to complete the Na'vi faces. The system allowed the actors to fully perform their parts, knowing that even their most subtle expressions would appear on the screen in the persona of their Na'vi characters.

# Aliens Above and Below

A 1979 film called *Alien* tells the story of spaceship crew being stalked and killed by a mysterious creature aboard their vessel. Warrant Officer Ripley, played by Sigourney Weaver, becomes the lone survivor who finally kills the alien. But Ripley was not finished with outer space horror: in a sequel called *Aliens*, Cameron would put Ripley in jeopardy once more.

Executives at Twentieth Century Fox were impressed with *The Terminator* and chose Cameron to write and direct the *Alien* sequel. Cameron insisted that Weaver reprise her role as Ripley, and in September 1985 filming began at Pinewood Studios in England. Conflicts soon arose with the British crew, whom Cameron characterized as "lazy, insolent, and arrogant."[45] Particularly infuriating was a union rule that required halting production twice a day for the traditional English teatime. Despite tension between Cameron and the crew, the actors found Cameron unexpectedly considerate of their work. "Jim never told the actors how to act," recalls actress Jeanette Goldstein. "He would always tell us, 'I know you know who the character is.' The choices in the film were the actors' choices."[46] Weaver's character, Ripley, was another strong Cameron woman but also displayed a motherly tenderness toward eleven-year-old Newt, a child left orphaned by the film's aliens. Once more, Ripley battled the vicious alien, saving herself and Newt. Produced for $18 million, *Aliens* grossed $80 million at the box office and received generally positive reviews.

In his next film, *The Abyss*, Cameron turned his attention from space to the deep sea. Based on a short story he wrote when he was seventeen, *The Abyss* tells of an encounter with nonterrestrial entities by the crew of an underwater oil rig as they help a navy rescue mission of a sunken US submarine. It was one of the director's most difficult and dangerous films to shoot. To capture believable underwater shots, Cameron leased an abandoned nuclear power plant in South Carolina, filming in a 7.5 million-gallon (28.4 million L) containment vessel. Rather than using stunt people, Cameron had his actors take diving lessons so they could perform their own underwater scenes. Cameron himself donned diving gear and often spent more than twelve hours a day directing the submerged action. At one point during filming, Cameron ran out of air and had to struggle to the surface. Thinking that the director was panicking, a safety diver tried to prevent Cameron from ascending too quickly, which could rupture his lungs, killing him. Close to blacking out and drowning, Cameron finally punched the safety man and made it to the surface.

One of the most spectacular special effects in *The Abyss* was the "pseudopod," a computer-generated alien entity resembling a living column of water. With its reflections and undulating motion, water has been one of the most difficult elements to render as a special effect. Cameron's vision of the pseudopod was brought to life by George Lucas's Industrial Light and Magic. In addition to being a believable water creature, the pseudopod, existing only as computer bits, was able to interact with the actors. At one point a character pokes her finger at the pseudopod, which reacts realistically to the touch. On the screen for only five minutes, the pseudopod was hailed by the *New York Times* as "a cinematic breakthrough."[47] It was a pioneering effort in computer-generated imagery (CGI) that paved the way for its use in films of all genres.

## The World of Avatar

Eighteen years after the release of *The Abyss*, Cameron took CGI to a whole new level with his science fiction masterpiece, *Avatar*. "I love science fiction," Cameron notes. "I love the idea of creating another world—another ecosystem of amazing creatures."[48] The world he created for his 2009 film *Avatar* was the far-off moon Pandora and its inhabitants, the primitive Na'vi, 10-foot-tall (3 m) humanoids. Pandora was a lush world filled with glowing trees, mountains that floated in the sky, and strange animals that flew, galloped, and lumbered through the rain forest. Humans lived

*In Avatar, Cameron created an alien world inhabited by the blue-skinned Na'vi. Mimicking how audiences identify with characters on-screen, Cameron gave the humans of his story the ability to walk among the Na'vi by remotely controlling genetically designed Na'vi avatars.*

# James Cameron and NASA

As a director, James Cameron creates new worlds and strange creatures for the entertainment of science fiction fans worldwide. But he also has a serious interest in real-life space travel and has lent his filmmaking expertise to NASA, America's space agency. Author Rebecca Keegan recounts Cameron's connection to NASA:

In 2002, the director became a member of the NASA Advisory Council, an independent civilian board that offers input to the NASA administrator. This put him at a table beside men such as astronauts Buzz Aldrin and John Glenn, and a cadre of renowned scientists and engineers. He also helped design a 3-D HD camera to go on future Mars missions. Cameron's main function at NASA has been to guide the agency in telling its own story better and to serve as a kind of motivational speaker for its scientists and engineers. . . .

In a 2005 speech to aerospace professionals in Orlando, Florida, Cameron entreated NASA to showcase the passion of its scientists and to let ordinary people get to know them, identify with them, and experience space travel vicariously through them. "There are six billion of us here on the ground who are not gonna get to go and a handful of us who will," he said. "Those who go become the avatars for the rest, the eyes and ears, the hearts and spirits for the rest of humanity."

Rebeca Keegan, *The Futurist: The Life and Films of James Cameron.* New York: Crown, 2009, pp. 223–24.

on Pandora by mentally inhabiting avatars, or Na'vi lookalikes, controlled by human thoughts. A $230 million budget allowed Cameron to create the alien world in *Avatar* down to the smallest detail. He hired a linguist to develop a real language of some one thousand words for the Na'vi. Artists carefully designed every plant, tree, insect, and animal on Pandora to avoid any resemblance to an earthly environment, at the same time basing each living object on the laws of natural science.

## Action and Conscience

But *Avatar* was more than beautiful landscapes and exotic creatures. For this film, Cameron wanted to "do something that has a conscience, that maybe in the enjoying it makes you think a little bit about the way you interact with nature and your fellow man."[49] In *Avatar*, a ruthless corporation from Earth is eager to destroy the habitat of the Na'vi to mine a rare element on Pandora. Scenes of helicopter-like combat ships annihilating the Na'vi's home and troops in mechanical exoskeletons fighting Na'vi warriors armed only with bows and arrows add action to the film. With the help of the film's hero who joins the Na'vi, the greedy corporate warriors are ultimately defeated and sent back to Earth. Critic Roger Ebert noted that *Avatar* "has a flat-out Green and anti-war message."[50]

Before *Avatar*, Cameron's 1997 film *Titanic* was the all-time box-office champion, grossing nearly $2.2 billion worldwide and earning Cameron an Academy Award for Best Director. *Avatar* dethroned the high-seas disaster film, bringing in more than $2.7 billion.

Cameron has maintained his lifelong curiosity about the world, and his successful films have given him the funds to explore new frontiers. Cameron's research for *The Abyss* and *Titanic* helped prepare him for a historic undersea voyage. In 2012 he took the first solo trip to the Challenger Deep, the deepest part of the Earth's oceans. During his two and a half hours on the bottom in the submersible *Deepsea Challenger*, he shot video and collected samples of soil and deep sea creatures for future study. Cameron has expressed interest in making future deep sea dives.

The future also holds more sci-fi adventures for Cameron. Three *Avatar* sequels, as well as two more *Terminator* films, are in various stages of production. Although he may be most remembered for *Titanic*, for fans of science fiction cinema, *The Terminator*, *Aliens*, *The Abyss*, and *Avatar* mark Cameron as one of the most creative and innovative science fiction directors.

## CHAPTER 5     Christopher Nolan

T he NASA Apollo program that put the first men on the moon in 1969 was a great achievement for humanity. But several trips back to the moon during the 1970s made clear that it was a lifeless orb. Beyond the moon, Mars holds the possibility of extraterrestrial life, but manned missions to the Red Planet are still years away.

For those who yearned to experience space travel, science fiction was the next best thing. With the release of *Star Wars* in 1977, sci-fi fans could experience the excitement and grandeur of space for the price of a movie ticket. Such films motivated many youngsters to pursue careers in space science, engineering, and even filmmaking. One young man who chose the path of science fiction cinema was Christopher Nolan.

## A Budding Filmmaker

Born in London, England, in 1970 to an English father and an American mother, Nolan divided his early years between living in London and Chicago. The Nolan family included older brother Matthew, born in 1969, and eventually their younger brother, Jonathan, born in 1976. Nolan was just seven years old when George

Lucas's *Star Wars* hit the theaters. His father took him to see the film, and from that moment he was hooked on science fiction and movies. "By the time I was 10 or 11," Nolan recalls, "I knew I wanted to make films."[51] His first attempts at creating his own sci-fi movies came courtesy of his father's Super 8 camera. Nolan and his older brother made a series of films called *Space Wars*, using *Star Wars* action figures. Nolan's uncle, who worked in the Apollo program at NASA, sent him film footage of rockets blasting off, which he incorporated into his movies. "I re-filmed them off the screen," says Nolan, "and cut them in, thinking no one would notice."[52] Nolan considers *Space Wars* his first step on the road to creating feature films.

> "By the time I was 10 or 11 I knew I wanted to make films."[51]
>
> —Christopher Nolan

## Influences

Nolan's interest in filmmaking influenced his choice for college. He attended the University College London (UCL), where he studied English literature. But what attracted him to UCL was its filmmaking facilities, where he graduated to making sixteen-millimeter films. "It was pretty obvious," Matthew Tempest, a college friend, remembers, "to anyone at the University College London film society in the early 1990s . . . that Chris Nolan was going places."[53] In 1989 he made his first real short film called *Tarantella*, which eventually aired on *Image Union*, a Chicago public television program featuring the works of independent filmmakers. While at UCL, Nolan met Emma Thomas, a fellow film enthusiast who would become his producing partner as well as his wife. After graduating in 1993, Nolan continued to hang around the film society, using its equipment to make two more short films: *Larceny* in 1995 and *Doodlebug* in 1997. To make ends meet, Nolan spent his days directing corporate films.

Although Nolan cites numerous influences on his career, he acknowledges that he was most inspired by the science fiction films of Stanley Kubrick (*2001: A Space Odyssey*) and Ridley Scott (*Alien* and *Blade Runner*). Also influential on Nolan's future work were Steven Spielberg's *Close Encounters of the Third*

When he was young, Christopher Nolan was fascinated with Star Wars. He even borrowed his father's Super 8 camera to shoot his own home movies that utilized Star Wars action figures to tell new stories. He credits these early films as the stepping-stones toward his current features.

*Kind* and the James Bond film *The Spy Who Loved Me*. Nolan explains the effect these films had on him: "Movies become indistinguishable from our own memories. You file them away and they become very personal."[54] Nolan's first feature film was based on a very personal experience.

## First Feature Films

Nolan's first independent feature film was 1998's *Following*. The idea of the film, in which a young man follows strangers on the streets of London, came from the trauma of having his apartment burglarized. "There is an interesting connection," Nolan explains, "between a stranger going through your possessions, and the concept of following people at random through a crowd—both take you beyond the boundaries of normal social relations."[55]

Nolan not only wrote and directed the film but also was the cinematographer and editor. His use of black-and-white film and natural lighting lent a dark, edgy quality to *Following*, an example of film noir—a genre of gritty crime films that were popular during the 1940s and 1950s.

Nolan's next feature was another independent noir film, *Memento*, written by his younger brother, Jonathan. *Memento* broke with traditional film structure by encompassing two threads: a black-and-white story that unfolds chronologically alternating with color sequences that develop in reverse time order. Shooting the film taught Nolan some important lessons in directing. "I learned lots of things on *Memento*," Nolan recalls, "but one thing I've always adhered to since then is letting actors perform as many takes as they want. . . . If an actor tells me they can do something more with a scene, I give them the chance, because it's not going to cost that much time."[56]

Released in 2000, the film earned more than $25 million domestically. At about the same time, a comic-book hero was ready to be given another chance to shine on the big screen.

> "One thing I've always adhered to . . . is letting actors perform as many takes as they want. . . . If an actor tells me they can do something more with a scene, I give them the chance, because it's not going to cost that much time."[56]
>
> —*Christopher Nolan*

## Nolan's Dark Knight Trilogy

The DC Comics character Batman had a long history in visual media, beginning with two serials in the 1940s and including a popular 1960s television show. Beginning in 1989, a series of four feature films had several different actors playing Batman. By the time the fourth film, *Batman and Robin*, was released in 1997, fans had grown tired of the franchise and plans for further Batman movies were shelved.

Warner Brothers decided to reboot the Batman franchise in 2003 and tapped Nolan as director. "I grew up with Batman," Nolan said upon being chosen. "I've been fascinated by him, and I'm excited to contribute to the lore of the character."[57] Nolan cowrote and directed three films that would become known as the Dark Knight trilogy: *Batman Begins* (2005), *The Dark Knight* (2008), and *The Dark Knight Rises* (2012). Under Nolan's influence, Batman became less of a comic book character and more of a complex and vulnerable human being trying to cope with life's tragedies: the Caped Crusader transformed into the Dark Knight. "From the beginning," says Nolan, "my interest was in taking on a super hero story but grounding it in reality."[58]

Nolan was also interested in the reality of the filming process itself. Rather than relying heavily on CGI, he planned most stunts to be done live for the camera. Nolan also rejected the filmmaker's standard practice of saving money by using a separate crew (called the second unit) to film certain scenes while the main photography is taking place. "If I don't need to be directing [all] the shots that go in the movie," he explains, "why do I need to be there at all? . . . So it all comes back to the question of defining what a director does. Each of us works in different ways. It's really helped me keep more of my personality in these big films."[59]

During a midnight showing of *The Dark Knight Rises* in Aurora, Colorado, in 2012, a heavily armed gunman stormed the theater, killing twelve moviegoers and wounding seventy. In a statement after the shooting, Nolan expressed "profound sorrow at the senseless tragedy that has befallen the entire Aurora community. . . . The movie theatre is my home, and the idea that someone would violate that innocent and hopeful place in such an unbearably savage way is devastating to me."[60]

## The Reality of Dreams

Between filming the second and third movies in the Dark Knight trilogy, Nolan directed a unique science fiction film. Instead of an outer space adventure with spaceships and aliens, Nolan decided to explore the inner space of the human mind. Nolan had come up with the idea of making a film about dreams ten years before he directed his sci-fi debut entitled *Inception*. Initially envisioning the movie as a low-budget production, Nolan eventually decided his ideas required something more elaborate. "It's intimate and

# Blockbuster and Cult Director

Christopher Nolan's films ring up blockbuster numbers at the box office, but they also become the subjects of intense scrutiny by fans who turn such works as *Interstellar* into objects of cult fascination. Journalist Gideon Lewis-Kraus examines this seeming contradiction in the *New York Times Magazine:*

> That his films manage to be both mainstream blockbusters and objects of such cult appeal is what makes Nolan a singular, and singularly admired, figure in Hollywood. He is commonly found sharing discriminating sentences of praise with James Cameron on the one hand and Paul Thomas Anderson [a director of character-driven films] on the other; he has been anointed, without any apparent campaigning on his own behalf, the successor of both Steven Spielberg and Stanley Kubrick. His loyalists have consistently and strenuously defended him against critics who claim that although he may be a masterful technician, he's not a visionary or true auteur. Regardless of the visionary question, however, it's pretty much impossible to think of a film that grossed more than a billion dollars and is better than "The Dark Knight"—or, to think of it in the way that Nolan prefers, a better film that was seen, so many times over, by so many people.

Gideon Lewis-Kraus, "The Exacting, Expansive Mind of Christopher Nolan," *New York Times Magazine*, October 30, 2014. www.nytimes.com.

emotional," he states, "but I realized I had this concept that lent itself to an epic-scale movie."[61] The film centers around the idea of implanting ideas into the minds of people while they sleep. "What 'Inception' deals with," Nolan explains, "is a science fiction concept in which really only one simple thing has changed, which is that you and I are able to experience the same dream at the same time."[62]

In *Inception*, a team of thieves infiltrates a businessman's dreams to plant an idea that will change the world's economic future. The movie is filled with special effects that take place in multilevel dreams, including a gravity-defying fight scene and a freight train barreling down a city street. As with his Batman films, Nolan created the effects live during shooting. The fight scene, for example, takes place in a hotel corridor that was built as a huge rotating set inspired by Kubrick's revolving drum set for *2001: A Space Odyssey*.

As with all of his films, Nolan directed *Inception* dressed in a crisp blue blazer and dress shirt, an unusual attire for a modern-day film director. It is, Nolan says, a comfortable reminder of his days as a uniform-wearing student in boarding school as well as a way to relieve him of the decision of what to wear each day. Also constantly with him on the set is a flask of tea, a remnant of his English upbringing. As a director, Nolan is well suited to a complex film like *Inception*. Veteran actor Michael Caine, who has appeared in six of Nolan's films, says that Nolan "belongs to an elite group of directors who can direct both action *and* actors. Here you have a director who can do both, which is very rare."[63]

*Inception* became both a blockbuster hit and an object of cult fascination, the latter due to the film's bewildering layers of dreams and a final scene that left moviegoers puzzling over its ambiguous meaning. In Nolan's next science fiction film, *Interstellar,* he took moviegoers on a spectacular ride through space and time.

> "[Nolan] belongs to an elite group of directors who can direct both action *and* actors. Here you have a director who can do both, which is very rare."[63]
>
> —*Actor Michael Caine*

## Traveling in Interstellar Space

While *Inception* plays with the idea of multilayered dreams, *Interstellar* centers on the distortion of time. The film is set in a near-future world where extensive crop failure has left the people of Earth starving and on the brink of extinction. An astronaut named Cooper leads an expedition to find a new home for humanity, leaving his young daughter behind. The voyage takes Cooper and his team to distant planets near a massive black hole, which distorts time and space. Through this time warp, Cooper communicates to his now-grown daughter, giving her information that will save the human race.

*Christopher Nolan wanted* Interstellar *to reflect up-to-date space science so that the forecasted events in the movie would be as accurately portrayed as possible. He also hoped this film about space exploration would spark interest in young viewers to become astronauts.*

In 2012 Nolan was chosen to direct the film, which he re-wrote from a script by his brother Jonathan. With *Interstellar*, he wanted to recapture the thrill of manned spaceflight during his youth. "I grew up at a time when to be an astronaut was the highest ambition of any child," he says. "I felt that had fallen off

# Creating a Wormhole

Traveling from Earth to another star or galaxy would mean an incredibly long voyage, some tens to hundreds of thousands of years just to reach the star nearest Earth. In the movie *Interstellar*, astronaut Cooper travels to a distant galaxy via a wormhole, a fold in the fabric of space. Nolan asked Kip Thorne, the film's science adviser, to make such a theoretical entity believable, as related by journalist Adam Rogers in *Wired* magazine.

> Back in 1983, when [physicist Carl] Sagan needed a plausible solution to this problem for the story that would become the movie *Contact*, Thorne suggested the wormhole, a hypothetical tear in the universe connecting two distant points via dimensions beyond the four we experience as space and time. A wormhole was a natural choice for *Interstellar* too. As Thorne talked about the movie with Nolan, their discussions about the physical properties of wormholes led to an inevitable question for a filmmaker: How do we show one onscreen? . . .
>
> [Special effects artist Paul Franklin] asked Thorne to generate equations that would guide their effects software the way physics governs the real world. . . . Franklin's team wrote new rendering software based on these equations and spun up a wormhole. It was like a crystal ball reflecting the universe, a spherical hole in spacetime. "Science fiction always wants to dress things up, like it's never happy with the ordinary universe," he [Franklin] says. "What we were getting out of the software was compelling straight off."

*Wired*, "How Building a Black Hole for *Interstellar* Led to an Amazing Scientific Discovery," October 2014. www.wired.com.

greatly in the last couple of decades."[64] Scientific accuracy was a key element of the film, especially since the concepts of black holes and time distortion are difficult to grasp. Nolan met with theoretical physicist Kip Thorne, discussing how such obscure ideas could be accurately portrayed on the screen. Thorne recalls that "the goal of having a movie in which science is embedded in the fabric from the beginning—and it's great science—that was preserved."[65]

# Filming the Future

Despite the highly technical subject of *Interstellar*, Nolan remained true to his own traditional methods of directing. Even with a budget of more than $160 million, he kept his takes to a minimum and filmed a large number of camera setups each day. Rather than using CGI for his spaceships, his team built highly detailed models, including the main spacecraft, a unique ring-shaped vehicle named *Endurance*. By the time *Interstellar* was shot, most Hollywood directors had switched from film to digital video as their production medium. Nolan, however, has resisted the trend. "For the last 10 years, I've felt increasing pressure to stop shooting film and start shooting video, but I've never understood why. It's cheaper to work on film, it's far better looking, it's the technology that's been known and understood for a hundred years, and it's extremely reliable."[66] Nolan has also resisted the movement toward 3-D films, which brings in additional revenue to the studios through the rental of 3-D glasses. "The question of 3-D is a very straightforward one," says Nolan. "I never met anyone who actually likes the format. . . . I certainly don't want to shoot in a format just to charge people a higher ticket price."[67]

Nolan does not need gimmicks to get audiences to see his movies. His films have made a total of more than $4 billion worldwide, making Nolan the fifth-highest-grossing director in cinema history. Having matured as a filmmaker from his first short Super 8 films to his latest blockbuster, Nolan still recalls the thrill of making his first big-budget film, *Memento*. "I got paid to direct it, I had millions of dollars in trucks, and hundreds of people and everything, and I haven't looked back since."[68]

> "I grew up at a time when to be an astronaut was the highest ambition of any child. I felt that had fallen off greatly in the last couple of decades."[64]
>
> —Christopher Nolan

He is, however, looking forward. Nolan rejoined the world of Batman as the executive producer of 2016's *Batman v Superman: Dawn of Justice*, and he is working on a new project for a possible 2017 release. Although it is still unclear if this new project will be another science fiction film, his legions of fans anxiously anticipate the next mind-bending film from Nolan's fertile imagination.

# CHAPTER 6

# J.J. Abrams

I t has never been easier to make a film than it is in the twenty-first century. High-definition video can now be shot with smartphones, tablets, and even still cameras. In the years before video, however, amateur filmmaking was more difficult. Shooting on film required a long wait for developing before the footage could be viewed, and editing meant physically cutting and splicing the film. Such difficulties did not discourage numerous young directors such as Steven Spielberg and George Lucas, who had a passion for telling stories on eight-millimeter film. J.J. Abrams, another young filmmaker, began making movies at the age of eight, using a borrowed Super 8 camera. Abrams would later pay tribute to young filmmakers in a sci-fi movie called *Super 8*. By then, his reputation as one of the bright young directors of Hollywood's so-called Super 8 Generation had been firmly established.

## Early Life

Jeffrey Jacob Abrams was born on June 27, 1966, in New York City. Jeffrey's parents, Gerald and Carol, called their baby son J.J., a nickname that he still goes by. J.J.'s father was a television network account executive who moved his family to Los Angeles in

1971, where he began a career as a television producer. His mother sold real estate and earned a law degree before also becoming a producer.

Abrams recalls being a precocious child. "I remember being taught to read at a very early age," he says. "Like creepy young. I remember being in the crib reading. My parents were very impressed."[69] His elementary school teachers, however, were not so charmed with what they considered his odd behavior. Abrams would often view other children on the playground through circled fingers, creating a make-believe camera viewfinder. Even at this young age, he displayed the eye of a future filmmaker, discovering the visual phenomenon of parallax; when panning his fingers back and forth, he noticed that "the foreground moved faster than the background."[70]

Unlike many sci-fi directors who devoured superhero comics growing up, Abrams says he "was never really a comic book fanatic."[71] He had many other interests as a youth, but magic especially intrigued him. Abrams performed tricks at school and at friends' birthday parties. "There was something about magic, about seeing that little disbelief in their eyes. I loved creating any kind of illusions."[72] He soon came to realize that movie directors were also magicians of sorts: they could make things appear and vanish on the screen.

> "I became incredibly comfortable and familiar with that world [of film production], so it never felt like anything but second nature to be on a set. Even as a little kid, all I ever wanted to do was be one of those guys on any level."[73]
>
> —J.J. Abrams

When Abrams was eight years old, his grandfather took him on a tour of Universal Studios. Seeing the magic of Hollywood close-up was all it took to get Abrams hooked on movies. "I became incredibly comfortable and familiar with that world," Abrams recalls, "so it never felt like anything but second nature to be on a set. Even as a little kid, all I ever wanted to do was be one of those guys on any level."[73]

# Filming in Super 8

When Abrams was about thirteen years old, he received a gift that he had been pestering his grandfather for: his own Super 8 camera. In his early films, Abrams experimented with various visual techniques. "Most of my first movies," Abrams recalls, "were excuses to test things out: primitive visual effects . . . testing out makeups on my family and friends, or doing fight scenes or chases."[74] Abrams wrote letters to Hollywood special effects artists to learn how they created their movie magic. In time, his films progressed from experiments to films that had a narrative story, written by Abrams himself. In 1981 fifteen-year-old Abrams screened his Super 8 films on a local television show in Los Angeles. Abrams's Super 8 films were also showcased at a film festival called the Best Teen Super 8mm Films of '81.

During his teen years at Palisades High School in Los Angeles, Abrams continued to make Super 8 films. He also enjoyed composing music (he wrote the score for the film *Nightbeast* when he was sixteen) and writing screenplays. When Abrams graduated in 1984, he wanted to study film at the University of Southern California, where many famous directors had gotten their education. But his father had a different idea.

# College and Beyond

Gerald Abrams felt that an education that exposed students to the world around them would be better for his son than a school with a narrower, film-based curriculum. "My father immediately advised me to go and learn what to make movies about, not just how to make movies."[75] Abrams chose Sarah Lawrence College, a distinguished liberal arts institution in Westchester County, New York, some 3,000 miles (4,828 km) from Abrams's California home.

Abrams kept writing scripts at Sarah Lawrence, and in his senior year he cowrote a script that was purchased by Disney and released in 1990 under the title *Taking Care of Business*. It was Abrams's first professional sale, and when he returned to California after graduation, more sales followed. Abrams wrote *Regarding Henry*, a film starring Harrison Ford, and *Forever Young*, a Mel Gib-

*As a youth, J.J. Abrams was intrigued by stage magic and often performed tricks for friends and family. As he got older, he learned that filmmaking involved a certain magic, the ability to create illusions and amaze audiences. Thus, he felt well-suited to choosing that as his career.*

son picture. Warner Brothers paid Abrams $2 million for the *Forever Young* script, the most ever paid for a screenplay at that time.

The next step in Abrams's career was television, where he created and wrote for the popular series *Felicity*, *Alias*, and *Lost*. Thanks to his extensive television credits, in 2004 Abrams was

# Restoring Spielberg's Films

In 1982 J.J. Abrams received an unexpected and startling phone call. It came from Steven Spielberg's assistant, who had a job proposal for Abrams and his friend Matt Reeves. Abrams describes his encounter with the great director's early work:

> We received a call from Steven's office after an article about the [Best Teen Super 8mm Films of '81] festival appeared in the LA Times. His assistant . . . asked us if we would be interested in repairing the films Steven had made when he was our age. Of course we were convinced this was a prank phone call, and to this day it makes no sense to me why Steven would put the original prints of *Firelight* and *Escape to Nowhere* in the hands of two fifteen-year-old strangers. I mean, have you ever seen 15-year-olds? Don't give them things if you want them back. Especially repaired. But Matt and I did it. In 1982 it was especially rare, if not impossible, to have access to the early works of a director, let alone Steven Spielberg's. But while his films were, of course, far better than ours, it was an inspiration to see how he began.

Quoted in Richard Corliss, "'What the Hell Would Spielberg Do Here?': J.J. Abrams Talks *Super 8*," *Time*, June 6, 2011. http://time.com.

offered the job of writing the script for the sci-fi movie *War of the Worlds*, directed by Steven Spielberg and starring Tom Cruise. Abrams was too busy with his television projects to accept the offer, and he worried that turning down two Hollywood superstars would end his filmmaking dream. "I felt like I had just committed career suicide,"[76] he explains. But Cruise was impressed by Abrams's television show *Alias* and hired him to direct *Mission Impossible III*, the next installment in Cruise's hit movie franchise. With a budget of $150 million, the film was the most expensive project ever undertaken by a first-time director. With the success of *Mission Impossible III*, Abrams was ready to take on an even bigger Hollywood franchise.

## Where No One Has Gone Before

*Star Trek* is one of the most popular science fiction movie series of all time. Its ten films, spanning 1979 to 2002, earned nearly $2 billion worldwide. In 2006 Paramount asked Abrams to direct a new *Star Trek* film to bring new life to the series. As a lifelong *Star Wars* fan, Abrams was not sure he was the right man to direct a *Star Trek* movie. "When I watched the show as a kid," Abrams recalls, "there was a talky, somewhat static vibe that I got from it. I felt it was cold and impersonal and very intellectual."[77] Despite his misgivings, Abrams signed on to direct the new film, whose story tells how Kirk, Spock, and the other original crewmembers of the USS *Enterprise* first come together.

Production began in November 2007. To impart a realistic look to the film, Abrams used one of his trademark techniques: lens flares. Allowing stray light to enter the camera's lens creates bright streaks and blobs that, for Abrams, make films look more dramatic and visually unique. While most directors try to avoid lens flares, Abrams actually shined flashlights into the camera to create them—more than seven hundred by one count.

More than one thousand special effects were used in the film, including digitally created spaceships, debris-filled explosions, and imploding planets. Not all of the effects were high-tech ones, however. For a scene where characters are shown falling toward a planet's surface, Abrams came up with the idea of having the actors stand on huge mirrors while shooting the scene from above, with the mirrors reflecting the sky as background. It was a simple but ingenious trick that comes across flawlessly in the film. In scenes where the camera shudders at an offscreen explosion, it is not digital wizardry but Abrams shaking the camera with his hands.

## Super 8

If *Star Trek* was science fiction of the future, Abrams's next film harkened back to science fiction of the past—his own past as a youthful Super 8 filmmaker. Entitled, rather naturally, *Super 8*, the film is set in 1979 and follows a group of young teenagers as they make a movie about zombies. While filming at a deserted train station, a freight train crashes in a mass of flame and flying debris and an alien is unleashed and begins terrorizing the small Ohio town. Barely escaping with their lives, the young filmmakers attempt to find the alien, ultimately discovering the reason for its destructive ways.

Abrams worked with one of his idols, Steven Spielberg, who produced *Super 8*. "It was such a privilege to work with Steven," Abrams recalls. "We had countless story meetings . . . finally ending with him telling me, 'J.J. Go write.'"[78] Visually, Abrams wanted *Super 8* to have the feel of the 1970s but with modern sensibilities. "I didn't want the film to look like it was made in 1979, but I wanted it to look the way we *remember* films looking from 1979 . . . with visual and rhythmic motifs that allude to a different era of moviemaking."[79] Mystery was also a part of *Super 8*, from keeping details of the film hidden before it opened to Abrams's decision to not reveal the alien until late in the film. "I think the audience ought to have a sense of discovery," he says. "That's what was so magical about the movies for me as a kid."[80]

Although the film has its share of spectacular visual effects, the story is more about the kids than the alien, including a budding romance between the two main characters, Joe and Alice. Abrams elicited winning performances from his young cast, especially fourteen-year-old Joel Courtney, who had never acted before getting the film's starring role as Joe. "I hope that when people see the movie," Abrams said before *Super 8* was released, "what they'll see is that there's a heart to the story . . . [that] it's about these characters."[81]

The story certainly resonated with many film critics. *Time* magazine's Richard Corliss called *Super 8* "a terrific movie, bending and transcending the science fiction genre into a fable about the power of innocence."[82] With a box office total of over $126 million, audiences obviously agreed.

> "[*Super 8* is] a terrific movie, bending and transcending the science fiction genre into a fable about the power of innocence."[82]
>
> —Film critic Richard Corliss

## *Star Trek* Versus *Star Wars*

In the world of science fiction movie fandom, a gap has emerged between the two most popular sci-fi franchises. The most ardent

Actors Zachary Quinto (left) and Chris Pine portray a younger Spock and Captain Kirk in the new Star Trek movie series. Director J.J. Abrams was unsure how he would reinvigorate the franchise, which he felt was more talky and intellectual than action oriented.

enthusiasts pledge their loyalty to either *Star Trek* or *Star Wars*, and lively debates on the merits of their respective film universes abound online. This gap seemed impossible to bridge until Abrams made sci-fi history as the first director to helm both a *Star Trek* and a *Star Wars* film.

In 2012 Abrams signed on to direct the second *Star Trek* reboot film, *Star Trek: Into Darkness*. Building on Abrams's previous *Star Trek* movie, in the new film the crew of the *Enterprise* begins its five-year mission by battling a powerful foe bent on destroying Earth. After its release on May 17, 2013, the film grossed $229 million worldwide, a modest return on its $190 million budget, but less than Abrams's first *Star Trek* film.

Even before *Star Trek: Into Darkness* hit the theaters, it was announced that Abrams would also direct the first film of a *Star Wars* sequel trilogy. Being given the reins of an iconic

# The Mystery Box

On one of Abrams's trips with his grandfather to a New York magic store, he bought a sealed box with a large question mark and the words *Tannen's Magic Mystery Box* on the front. Most children would have ripped open the tantalizing box as soon as they got home, but Abrams kept it sealed. The mystery of what might be in the box was more appealing to him than actually seeing it. In a speech in March 2007, Abrams brought his mystery box onstage and talked about what it meant to him.

> Now, I was looking at this, it was in my office as it always is, and I was thinking, why have I not opened this? . . . And I realized that I haven't opened it because it represents something important—to me. It represents my grandfather. . . . But the thing is, that it [also] represents infinite possibility. It represents hope. It represents potential. And what I love about this box, and what I realize I sort of do in whatever it is that I do, is I find myself drawn to infinite possibility, that sense of potential. And I realize that mystery is the catalyst for imagination. . . .
>
> What's a bigger mystery box than a movie theater? You know? You go to the theater, you're just so excited to see anything. . . . And you're full of that amazing—that feeling of excited anticipation.

J.J. Abrams, "The Mystery Box," TED, March 2007. www.ted.com.

film franchise that has legions of loyal and demanding fans was, for Abrams, a scary prospect. "Frankly, taking this on is vaguely terrifying," he admits, "because you . . . hope the fans will like what you're doing. They deserve something great and we just work really hard to give it to them."[83] Commenting on the differences in the two classic science fiction series, Abrams says that "*Star Trek* in some ways . . . informed *Star Wars*. . . . They're such different worlds, though. The stories, the characters, the universes. One is sort of our future, much more towards science-based in theory, and 'Star Wars' is like a fairytale, but it happens to take place in space."[84]

*Star Wars: The Force Awakens* opened to great fanfare in December 2015. In its first twelve days it earned more than $1 billion worldwide, making it the first film to reach that mark in such a short time. The story takes place thirty years after *Return of the Jedi*, the third film of the original trilogy. The triumph over the Empire at the end of that film has not lasted, and the rebels, now called the Resistance, must battle a nemesis known as the First Order to restore peace. *The Force Awakens* introduces new heroes and villains to the *Star Wars* universe and brings back the revered characters of Luke Skywalker, Han Solo, and Princess Leia. Another new addition, BB-8, joins the popular droids R2-D2 and C-3PO. Visually, Abrams wanted his film to revisit the look of the original *Star Wars* trilogy. "There was a feeling," recalls scriptwriter Lawrence Kasdan, "that we wanted to have more of a slightly retro feeling—more tactile and less C.G.-oriented."[85] Still, special effects abound in *The Force Awakens*, from epic spaceship battles to fully realized computer-generated characters.

> "Frankly, taking [*Star Wars*] on is vaguely terrifying, because you . . . hope the fans will like what you're doing. They deserve something great and we just work really hard to give it to them."[83]
>
> —*J.J. Abrams*

With his *Star Wars* film completed, Abrams returned to *Star Trek*, producing the next sequel, *Star Trek Beyond*, which was set for release in 2016. It is expected that Abrams will produce yet another film, the fourteenth in the *Star Trek* franchise, slated tentatively for 2019. He is also producing a sequel to 2008's *Cloverfield*, a horror film that he produced that was directed by his boyhood friend Matt Reeves.

Many sci-fi film buffs divide themselves into either the *Star Wars* or *Star Trek* camps. But regardless of their cinematic loyalties, J.J. Abrams's fans are grateful for his devotion to carrying on the traditions of the two greatest science fiction film franchises of all time.

# SOURCE NOTES

## Introduction: The World of Science Fiction

1. Isaac Asimov, *Asimov on Science Fiction*. New York: Doubleday, 1982, p. 22.
2. Quoted in Adam Roberts, *Science Fiction: The New Critical Idiom*. London: Routledge, 2000, p. 61.

## Chapter 1: Steven Spielberg

3. Quoted in Joseph McBride, *Steven Spielberg: A Biography*. Jackson: University Press of Mississippi, 2010, pp. 47, 41.
4. Quoted in McBride, *Steven Spielberg*, pp. 54–55.
5. Quoted in McBride, *Steven Spielberg*, p. 133.
6. Quoted in Richard Schickel, *Steven Spielberg: A Retrospective*. New York: Sterling, 2012, p. 60.
7. Quoted in Roger Ebert, "Preview: *Close Encounters of the Third Kind*," November 13, 1977. www.rogerebert.com.
8. Quoted in Abigail Pogrebin, *Stars of David: Prominent Jews Talk About Being Jewish*. New York: Broadway, 2006, p. 25.
9. Quoted in Susan Goldman Rubin, *Steven Spielberg: Crazy for Movies*. New York: Abrams, 2001, p. 51.
10. Quoted in Schickel, *Steven Spielberg*, p. 91.

## Chapter 2: George Lucas

11. Quoted in Dale Pollock, *Skywalking: The Life and Films of George Lucas*. New York: Harmony, 1983, p. xvi.

12. John Baxter, *Mythmaker: The Life and Work of George Lucas*. New York: Spike, 1999, p. 44.
13. Quoted in Baxter, *Mythmaker*, p. 47.
14. Quoted in Pollock, *Skywalking*, p. 68.
15. Quoted in Pollock, *Skywalking*, p. 91.
16. Quoted in Marcus Hearn, *The Cinema of George Lucas*. New York: Abrams, 2005, p. 47.
17. Quoted in J.W. Rinzler, *The Making of Star Wars: The Definitive Story Behind the Original Film*. New York: Random House, 2007, p. 18.
18. Quoted in Pollock, *Skywalking*, p. 163.
19. Quoted in David Taylor, *How Star Wars Conquered the Universe: The Past, Present, and Future of a Multibillion Dollar Franchise*. New York: Basic, 2014, p. 153.
20. Quoted in Hearn, *The Cinema of George Lucas*, p. 89.
21. Quoted in Pollock, *Skywalking*, p. 185.
22. Quoted in Alan Dean Foster, *Splinter of the Mind's Eye*. New York: Ballantine, 1994.

# Chapter 3: Stanley Kubrick

23. Arthur C. Clarke, *2001: A Space Odyssey*. New York: Penguin, 1999, p. ix.
24. Quoted in Biography.com, "Stanley Kubrick." www.biography.com.
25. Quoted in Alexander Walker, *Stanley Kubrick, Director*. New York: Norton, 1999, p. 11.
26. Quoted in Vincent LoBrutto, *Stanley Kubrick: A Biography*. New York: Fine, 1997, p. 30.
27. Quoted in Walker, *Stanley Kubrick, Director*, p. 14.
28. Clarke, *2001*, p. xi.
29. Quoted in Eric Nordern, "*Playboy* Interview: Stanley Kubrick," in *Stanley Kubrick Interviews*, by Gene D. Phillips. Jackson: University Press of Mississippi, 2001, p. 47.
30. Piers Bizony, "Shipbuilding," in *The Making of "2001: A Space Odyssey,"* ed. Stephanie Schwam. New York: Random House, 2000, p. 43.
31. John Baxter, *Stanley Kubrick: A Biography*. New York: Carroll & Graf, 1997, p. 6.
32. Quoted in Jeremy Bernstein, "Profile: Stanley Kubrick," in Phillips, *Stanley Kubrick Interviews*, p. 43.
33. Quoted in Leonard F. Wheat, *Kubrick's 2001: A Triple Allegory*. Lanham, MD: Scarecrow, 2000, p. 160.
34. Quoted in LoBrutto, *Stanley Kubrick*, p. 312.

## Chapter 4: James Cameron

35. Quoted in Rebecca Keegan, *The Futurist: The Life and Films of James Cameron*. New York: Crown, 2009, p. 5.
36. Quoted in Marc Shapiro, *James Cameron: An Unauthorized Biography of the Filmmaker*. Los Angeles: Renaissance, 2000, p. 30.
37. Quoted in Joann Rhetts, "Writer-Director Shows the Special Effect Energy Can Radiate," in *James Cameron Interviews,* ed. Brent Dunham. Jackson: University Press of Mississippi, 2012, p. 17.
38. Quoted in Shapiro, *James Cameron*, p. 88.
39. Quoted in Kenneth Turan, "*Us*: James Cameron Interview," Terminator Files. www.terminatorfiles.com.
40. Quoted in Shapiro, *James Cameron*, p. 117.
41. Quoted in Shapiro, *James Cameron*, p. 120.
42. Quoted in Keegan, *The Futurist*, p. 53.
43. Quoted in Shapiro, *James Cameron*, p. 124.
44. Quoted in Shapiro, *James Cameron*, p. 115.
45. Quoted Keegan, *The Futurist*, p. 70.
46. Quoted in Shapiro, *James Cameron*, p. 142.
47. Quoted in Aljean Harmetz, "*The Abyss*: A Foray into Deep Waters," *New York Times,* August 6, 1989. www.nyt.com.
48. Quoted in Frank Rose, *The Art of Immersion*. New York: Norton, 2011, p. 48.
49. Quoted in *Telegraph*, "'*Avatar* Friday': Fans Will Be Shown Preview of James Cameron's 3-D Film," August 18, 2009. www.telegraph.co.uk.
50. Roger Ebert, "*Avatar,*" December 11, 2009. www.rogerebert.com.

## Chapter 5: Christopher Nolan

51. Quoted in Will Lawrence, "Christopher Nolan Interview for *Inception*," *Telegraph*, July 19, 2010. www.telegraph.co.uk.
52. Quoted in Andrew Purcell, "Christopher Nolan's Final Frontier." www.andrewpurcell.com.
53. Matthew Tempest, "I Was There at the Inception of Christopher Nolan's Film Career," *Guardian*, February 11, 2011. www.theguardian.com.
54. Quoted in *Wired*, "Deep Impact," December 2014, p. 84.
55. Quoted in uczccnw, "Christopher Nolan: Screenwriter and Director: The Man Behind the Mask," Library, Archive, & Information Studies: UCL Famous Alumni, December 8, 2008. http://wiki.ucl.ac.uk/display/SLAISFAlumni/Christopher+Nolan.

56. Quoted in Jeffrey Ressner, "The Traditionalist," *DGA Quarterly,* Spring 2012, Directors Guild of America. www.dga.org.

57. Quoted in *Variety*, "'Batman' Captures Director Nolan," January 28, 2003. www.variety.com.

58. Quoted in Jody Duncan Jesser and Janine Pourroy, *The Art and Making of the Dark Knight Trilogy*. New York: Abrams, 2012, p. 32.

59. Quoted in Ressner, "The Traditionalist."

60. Quoted in *Rolling Stone*, "'Dark Knight' Director Calls Aurora Shooting 'Unbearably Savage,'" July 21, 2012. www.rollingstone.com.

61. Quoted in *Telegraph*, "*Inception:* Christopher Nolan Interview," July 1, 2010. www.telegraph.co.uk.

62. Quoted in Dave Itzkoff, "A Man and His Dream: Christopher Nolan and 'Inception,'" *ArtsBeat* (blog), *New York Times,* June 30, 2010. www.artsbeat.blogs.nytimes.com.

63. Quoted in Jesser and Pourroy, *The Art and Making of the Dark Knight Trilogy*, p. 24.

64. Quoted in Ben Fritz, "Director Christopher Nolan Causes Stir While Promoting 'Interstellar' at Comic-Con," *Wall Street Journal*, July 24, 2014. www.wsj.com.

65. Quoted in Adam Rogers, "Wrinkles in Spacetime: The Warped Astrophysics of *Interstellar,*" *Wired*, October 2014. www.wired.com.

66. Quoted in Ressner, "The Traditionalist."

67. Quoted in David Germaine, "No 'Dark Knight' in 3D," *Salon*, July 17, 2012. www.salon.com.

68. Quoted in Ressner, "The Traditionalist."

# Chapter 6: J.J. Abrams

69. Quoted in *New York Times*, "J.J. Abrams: By the Book," October 24, 2013. www.nytimes.com.

70. Quoted in David Kamp, "What You Should Know About: J.J. Abrams: A Panoply of Eccentric Biographical Data Re: Filmdom's Premier Pop Auteur," *Vanity Fair*, June 2013. www.vanityfair.com.

71. Quoted in Vanessa Kaneshiro, "10 Questions for J.J. Abrams," *Time*, May 28, 2009. http://time.com.

72. Quoted in Scott Bowles, "J.J. Abrams Raises Curtain on Scary 'Super 8,'" *USA Today*, June 8, 2011. www.usatoday.com.

73. Quoted in Jake Coyle, "J.J. Abrams Finds the Big Screen," *Washington Post*, May 4, 2006. www.washingtonpost.com.

74. Quoted in Richard Corliss, "'What the Hell Would Spielberg Do Here?': J.J. Abrams Talks *Super 8*," *Time*, June 6, 2011. http://time.com.

75. Quoted in Chris Serico, "J.J. Abrams," Serico Stories. http://serico stories.tumblr.com.

76. Quoted in Jeff Jensen, "Steven Spielberg and J.J. Abrams Discuss How They Met and Reveal the True Origins of 'Super 8,'" *Entertainment Weekly*, June 9, 2011. www.ew.com.

77. Quoted in Brian D. Johnson, "The Man with *Star Wars* and *Star Trek* in His Hands," *Maclean's*, May 14, 2013. www.macleans.ca.

78. Quoted in Corliss, "'What the Hell Would Spielberg Do Here?'"

79. Quoted in Bowles, "J.J. Abrams Raises Curtain on Scary 'Super 8.'"

80. Quoted in Alex Billington, "Interview: Bad Robot's J.J. Abrams—Writer and Director of "Super 8," First Showing. www.firstshowing.net.

81. Quoted in Corliss, "'What the Hell Would Spielberg Do Here?'"

82. Quoted in Bauer Publishing, "The Force Awakens," *Life Story Movie Magic: Countdown to "Star Wars: The Force Awakens,"* 2015, p. 30.

83. Quoted in *Tavis Smiley*, "Writer-Producer-Director J.J. Abrams," PBS, September 24, 2013. www.pbs.org.

84. Quoted in *Tavis Smiley*, "Writer-Producer-Director J.J. Abrams."

85. Quoted in Bruce Handy, "The Daring Genesis of J.J. Abrams's *Star Wars: The Force Awakens*," *Vanity Fair,* May 31, 2015. www.vanity fair.com/hollywood/2015/05/star-wars-the-force-awakens-vanity -fair-cover.

# FOR FURTHER RESEARCH

## Books

Jody Duncan and Lisa Fitzpatrick, *The Making of "Avatar."* New York: Abrams, 2010.

Jacqueline Furby and Stuart Joy, eds., *The Cinema of Christopher Nolan: Imagining the Impossible*. New York: Columbia University Press, 2015.

Guy Haley, ed., and Stephen Baxter, *Sci-fi Chronicles: A Visual History of the Galaxy's Greatest Science Fiction*. Richmond Hill, Ontario, Canada: Firefly, 2014.

Rebecca Keegan, *The Futurist: The Life and Films of James Cameron*. New York: Crown, 2009.

Bill Krohn, *Stanley Kubrick*. Rev. ed. Paris: Cahiers du Cinéma Sarl, 2010.

Joseph McBride, *Steven Spielberg: A Biography*. Jackson: University Press of Mississippi, 2010.

Barbara Sheen, *J.J. Abrams*. Farmington Hills, MI: Lucent, 2015.

David Taylor, *How "Star Wars" Conquered the Universe: The Past, Present, and Future of a Multibillion Dollar Franchise*. New York: Basic, 2014.

## Internet Sources

Jeff Jensen, "Steven Spielberg and J.J. Abrams Discuss How They Met and Reveal the True Origins of 'Super 8,'" *Entertainment Weekly*, June 9, 2011. www.ew.com.

Tom Shone, "Christopher Nolan: The Man Who Rebooted the Blockbuster," *Guardian*, November 4, 2014. www.theguardian.com.

T.R. Witcher, "Kubrick's Indestructible Influence: 'Interstellar' Joins the Long Tradition of Borrowing from '2001,'" *Salon*, November 21, 2014. www.salon.com.

## Websites

**DreamWorks Studios (www.dreamworksstudios.com)**. This is the official website of Steven Spielberg's production company, with information on his previous and upcoming films.

**James Cameron Online (www.jamescamerononline.com)**. This fan website offers information about Cameron and his films. It includes interviews, a biography, and samples of Cameron's artwork.

**Star Wars (www.starwars.com)**. This comprehensive website showcases George Lucas's epic sci-fi saga and provides information and clips from all the *Star Wars* movies.

**Visual Memory: Stanley Kubrick (www.visual-memory.co.uk)**. This website contains links to websites about Stanley Kubrick, including a biography, frequently asked questions, and a site for *2001: A Space Odyssey*.

# INDEX

# PICTURE CREDITS

Cover: Depositphotos

6: Depositphotos

10: Depositphotos

14: Photofest Images

20: Depositphotos

25: Photofest Images

31: © Sunset Boulevard/Corbis

34: © Sunset Boulevard/Corbis

40: Photofest Images

45: Photofest Images

50: Photofest Images

55: Photofest Images

61: Depositphotos

65: Photofest Images

## ABOUT THE AUTHOR

Craig E. Blohm has written numerous books and magazine articles for young readers. He and his wife, Desiree, reside in Tinley Park, Illinois.